Armin Geo. Weng,
Bridgeport, Conn.

Feb. 8, 1927.

Bought at Wanamaker's,
Phila., while doing
research work for my Ph. D.

THE MINISTER AS SHEPHERD

BY

CHARLES EDWARD JEFFERSON

PASTOR OF THE BROADWAY TABERNACLE
IN NEW YORK CITY

NEW YORK
THOMAS Y. CROWELL COMPANY
PUBLISHERS

THE GEORGE SHEPARD

LECTURES ON PREACHING

At Bangor Theological Seminary

1912

CONTENTS

vii

THE MINISTER AS SHEPHERD

I

The Shepherd Idea in Scripture and History

OF all the titles which have been minted for the envoys of the Son of God, that of "shepherd" is the most popular, the most beautiful, and the most ample. Bishop, presbyter, preacher, priest, clergyman, rector, parson, minister, all of these have been long, and are still, in use, but not one of them is so satisfying or sufficient as "shepherd."

"Bishop" came into the church from the Gentile world, and was early set aside to designate a special grade of minister—thus losing the range of application which it formerly possessed. In the original sense of the word, bishop is one who oversees and superintends, and the head, therefore, of every congregation might be rightfully called a bishop. Such use of it under present conditions would be misleading.

Presbyter came into the church through Judaism. Because both the Jewish and Gentile worlds are reflected in our New Testament, presbyter and bishop stand side by side upon its pages. At the beginning, bishop and presbyter were synonymous titles, belonging to one and the same official. In time, however, the bishops of the local church dropped the title " bishop," that name being borne thereafter solely by the heads of dioceses or districts. Presbyter, the name retained by the head of the local congregation, carries on its face the idea of age. Only men of years could in the Jewish church be elders. In the Christian church age is not a prime qualification for office, or an essential possession of those who lead. The word "elder" does not emphasize that which is cardinal in Christian work; it calls attention to the years a man has lived rather than to the work which he has been called to do.

Priest is a title borrowed from both Judaism and Paganism, and around it ages of controversy have raged. It has always been contended by many that the idea of priest is foreign to the Christian religion, and that to call the head of a Christian church a priest is to introduce a conception which works mischief. It is significant that both Jesus and his apostles carefully eschew that word. Only sects or sections of the church of Christ to-day make use of it.

Preacher is also a sectional title confined to those limited areas of the Christian world in which preaching is considered the chief if not the only heaven-ordained work of an ambassador of Christ. The use of such a title implies that the head of a church is preëminently a speaker, and that in the act of speaking he is performing the crowning function of his office. Clergyman is a rather chilling name, fixing the mind not on the man's personality, but on his office.   Rector is to many a repellent title, magnifying as it does the idea of ruling, and carrying with it unpleasant reminiscences of days of monarchy when ecclesiastical leaders of despotic temper lorded it in lofty manner over the saints of God.

Parson, the favorite title of George Herbert and of many others, has in our modern world taken on a somewhat depreciatory color.   When men speak facetiously of the minister they usually call him "parson," with a familiar accent which patronizes and smiles.   The word parson is really the word person, and in times when the representative of the church was the one august and imperial person in the parish, there was a fitness in the title which it has long since lost.   In these democratic days when the minister has stepped down from off his pedestal, it is usually mock reverence which toys with the title "parson."   Parson has become a sort of joke.

Minister is, on the whole, a wider and more adequate title than any of the seven already mentioned, but it has the disadvantage of being the same title by which the State names the highest of its officials. When one speaks of the "minister," it is impossible from that word alone for the hearer to decide whether it is a minister of the church or a minister of the government to whom reference is made. One of the limitations of the name is its ambiguity, and another is its failure to discriminate. It does not distinguish the leader from his followers. It does not draw a line between the general and his soldiers. It is a word which belongs to every follower of Jesus. Servantship is of the essence of the Christian life. All Christians are ministers or servants. To speak of "the minister" is to imply that there is only one, whereas there ought to be as many as there are members of the church. One wonders sometimes whether the rank and file of our churches would not have been more zealous in ministering to one another and also to the community, if the name "minister" had not been monopolized by a single man. The exclusive use of the title seems to justify indolent church members in their habit of considering the pastor the only obligated worker in the parish.

But when we come to "shepherd," we reach a title without spot or wrinkle or any such thing. Here is a word which has come down through the centuries without loss of wealth of meaning and free from stain. It is the one title which is prized and reverenced in every fold of the great flock of Christ. In the Greek and Roman and Anglican communions, in the Lutheran, Reformed, and other great Christian bodies, Pastor is a name which gives no offense. Rome likes the word. Her priests in charge of churches are called " Pastors." The Church of England likes the word, she calls her rectors "Pastors." Churches which usually call their leaders ministers and preachers, call them also " Pastors," unwilling to part with so glorious a name. Pastor is a word understood around the

but he liked to think of himself as a shepherd. The shepherd idea was often in his mind. When he looked out upon the crowds in Galilee, they reminded him of sheep without a shepherd. He told men repeatedly that he had been sent to gather and save the lost sheep of the House of Israel. He considered his followers all sheep, and looking into the distance, he saw other sheep which also were his own. " Other sheep I have which are not of this fold, them also I must bring, and they shall hear my voice; and they shall become one flock, one shepherd." When he thought of himself in the world to come seated on a throne with all the nations assembled before him, even there he was still a shepherd, doing things which shepherds do.

Early in Hebrew history, the word shepherd had passed into a metaphor. The literal keeper of sheep was so prominent a character in those early days that he became a type of the highest servants of Jehovah, a symbol for the expression of lofty ideals of service. Fragrant memories gath-

ered round the word, and men poured into
it rare and precious meanings. A priest
was called a shepherd, and so also was a
prophet, and so also later on was a prince
or king. Every man in exalted place, entrusted with public responsibilities, was
crowned with the title "shepherd." So
beautiful was the figure and so rich its contents, that by and by somebody dared to
apply it even to God. Kings and princes,
priests and prophets, here on earth were
under-shepherds, and in the heavens there
was a shepherd over all—Jehovah. A poetic genius taught all his countrymen to
sing: "The Lord is my shepherd, I shall
not want." When the nation fell into difficulties and calamities overtook it, the saints
cried out: "Give ear, O Shepherd of Israel, Thou that leadest Joseph like a flock."
Before men dared to think of God as their
Father, they called him their Shepherd.
Divine shepherdhood was one of the steps
in the shining stairway up which the world
climbed to the idea of divine fatherhood.

But while there was a good shepherd in

the skies there was no good shepherd on the earth. All the shepherds of Israel, one after another, proved disappointing. They did not do their duty. They failed to feed the flock. They did not wisely guide it. They could not save it. But the Hebrew heart did not despair. It dared to dream of an ideal shepherd who would surely come. A Messiah had been promised, and he would be a shepherd. He would guide and feed and save the sheep. Through many generations this figure of the Shepherd-Messiah flitted before the minds of the seers of Israel. They painted him in colors which at last burned themselves into the retina of the nation's eyes. When they painted pictures of bad shepherds, they always hung up another picture, the picture of the shepherd who was good. When they wished to criticise an unworthy king or condemn an unfaithful priest, they compared him with the shepherd whom God had promised. It was this portrait of the good shepherd which sustained the nation's heart. " He will feed his flock like a shepherd. He will gather the lambs in his arms and carry them in his bosom, and will gently lead those that have their young." Thus did they contrast the Shepherd-Messiah with the shepherds who had been impatient and selfish and cruel. It was to men whose eyes were filled with this lovely picture and whose hearts were awed by this thrilling expectation, that Jesus spoke when he said: "I am the good shepherd. Thieves and robbers have preceded me, men who have done all the abominations which Ezekiel and Zechariah and others have narrated, but I am the good shepherd. I know every sheep by name. I give security and liberty and sustenance to all. I am going to lay down my life for the sheep." Jesus had many metaphors by which to image forth his character and his office, but the metaphor by which he loved best to paint his portrait was "shepherd."

As he chose this title for himself, so also did he give it to the leader of the apostles.

Peter was a fisherman, and could have best understood, presumably, the language native to a fisherman's lips, but Jesus in his final charge to the son of Jonas used only the vocabulary of the sheepfold. " Feed my lambs. Tend my sheep. Feed my sheep." In other words: " Be a shepherd, and do a shepherd's work." The great shepherd of the sheep in framing a charge which he deemed sufficient for the guidance and encouragement of the leaders of the Christian church down to the end of time, used only a shepherd's speech. The history of the church begins with Jesus saying to the leader who is to head the work of discipling the nations: "I am a shepherd, be thou a shepherd too."

Peter never forgot what the Lord said to him that morning down on the shore of the sea. Like the Master he looked at men henceforth always with a shepherd's eyes. " Ye were going astray like sheep," he writes to a company of his converts, " but are now returned unto the shepherd and bishop of your souls." It was the good shepherd who had found Peter, and who had given him his work. It is the good shepherd for whose return the apostle waits. The supreme shepherd is coming again, therefore Peter writes to the pastors of the churches: "Tend the flock of God which is among you. Make yourselves ensamples to the flock, and when the chief shepherd shall be manifested, ye shall receive the crown of glory that fadeth not away." Peter did all of his work, not under a great taskmaster's eye, but under the gentle and loving glance of the shepherd whose delight it is to seek and to save that which is lost.

Paul was not one of the original twelve. He never knew Jesus in the flesh, but he received from him in the spirit the idea of shepherding. Paul, like Peter, loved to think of himself as a shepherd. He looked upon men with the loving solicitude and searching affection of a shepherd's eyes. Every parish was to him a fold, and the

men in charge of the parish were shepherds. He speaks to the officers of the
church in Ephesus in the language of a
shepherd: "Take heed unto yourselves,
and to all the flock, to feed the church of
the Lord which he purchased with his
own blood. In all things I gave you an
example."

The shepherd idea, then, may be said to
color the entire New Testament world, to
permeate its atmosphere and to flow in its
blood. The generation of Christians which
was molded by the Apostles was trained to
think of Jesus as the Good Shepherd, and
the church leaders instructed by Peter and
Paul went forth as shepherds to feed and
tend Christ's sheep. It is a ruling idea of
the apostolic age which breaks into music
in the fullest-toned of all our New Testament benedictions: "Now the God of
Peace, who brought again from the dead
the great shepherd of the sheep with the
blood of an eternal covenant, even our Lord
Jesus, make you perfect in every good

thing to do his will, working in us that which is well pleasing in his sight, through Jesus Christ, to whom be glory forever and ever. Amen." This is the benediction which the New Testament pronounces over all Christian workers, and it has a special significance for men who are fitting themselves for service in the Christian ministry. It is through the great shepherd of the sheep that God perfects men for the doing of his will. It is by building up in them a shepherd's disposition and imparting to them a shepherd's skill that he enables them to do that which is well pleasing in his sight. If the aim of our life is to be Christ-like, then we must be like a shepherd. If we are called to fulfil Christ's mission, then our work is that of a shepherd. If we are to be judged by Christ, then the standard of the judgment day is to be the standard of a shepherd. Since Christ is the image of his Father, it follows that God himself is a shepherd God. To glorify him we must do a shepherd's work, and to enjoy

est experiences, in what form he comforted them in their most solemn hours. It was the tenderness of the shepherd which soothed them when their hearts were bleeding. It was the shepherd's courage and strength which braced them in the day of persecution and in the hour of death. Christianity was at first the religion of the good shepherd. To the men of the second century the Saviour of the world was a keeper of sheep. As Dean Stanley says, " The kindness, the courage, the grace, the love, the beauty of the good shepherd was to them prayer book and articles, creed and canons, all in one. They looked on that figure and it conveyed to them all that they wanted. As ages passed on, the good shepherd faded away from the mind of the Christian world, and other emblems of the Christian faith have taken his place. Instead of the gracious and gentle pastor, there came the omnipotent Judge, or the crucified Sufferer, or the infant in his mother's arms, or the Master in his parting supper, or the figures of innumerable saints and angels, or the elaborate expositions of the various forms of theological controversy. There is hardly any allusion to the good shepherd in Athanasius or in Jerome. There is hardly any in the Summa Theologiæ of Thomas Aquinas, none in the Tridentine catechism, none in the Thirty-nine Articles, none in the Westminster Confession."

When church leaders began to lose the vision of the good shepherd, they at the same time began to drift away from the New Testament ideal of ministerial service. Little by little they magnified their office in ways not sanctioned by the good shepherd of the sheep. They became priests offering a bloodless sacrifice, they assumed the functions of rulers, making a specialty of law and discipline. They degenerated into tyrants, setting themselves up as sole custodians of the grace of God, claiming sovereignty not only over the kingdoms of this world, but also over the

vast empire of the dead. The church lost
the way which leads to life as soon as the
envoys of the Son of God forgot that they
were shepherds. Darkness fell upon the
earth when the shepherd was swallowed up
in the priest.

But an ideal, once apprehended, never
fades completely from the mind of the
world. The church has never surrendered
entirely her belief in Jesus as the Shepherd
Saviour, and has never given up altogether
her feeling that ministers ought to be shepherds of the sheep. The shepherd idea
has something in it which appeals to the
universal heart. Even in our western
world from which machinery and commerce
have driven the shepherd and his flock, the
best-loved of all the Psalms remains the
Shepherd Psalm. More men and women
read and cherish " The Lord is my shepherd, I shall not want," than any other
poem in the Psalter. Millions who have
had no experience with sheepfolds, and to
whom a sheep has been an animal almost

unknown, have been strangely moved by the piercing pathos of the story which Jesus told of a shepherd who went out in search of one sheep that was lost. What Christian song went deeper into the heart of the nineteenth century than " There were ninety and nine that safely lay in the shelter of the fold " as sung by Mr. Sankey round the world. Congregations every Sunday sing:

> " Saviour, like a shepherd lead us,
>   Much we need thy tender care;
> In thy pleasant pastures feed us;
>   For our use thy folds prepare,"—

and also this:

> " In tenderness he sought me,
>   Weary and weak with sin;
> And on his shoulders brought me
>   Back to his fold again,"—

and also this:

> " The King of love my Shepherd is,
>   Whose goodness faileth never;
> I nothing lack if I am his
>   And he is mine forever."

Into the prayers as well as the hymnology, the shepherd idea has been inextricably woven. Multitudes of hearts find relief in making the confession: "We have erred and strayed from thy ways like lost sheep. We have followed too much the devices and desires of our own hearts." The devout heart drops unconsciously into such phrases as "All we like sheep have gone astray: we have turned every one to his own way, and Jehovah hath laid on him the iniquity of us all." The spirit in us, helping our infirmities, teaches us to cry out: "O thou great shepherd of the sheep! Guide us, feed us, save us ever more!"

It is necessary only to walk through any of the great European picture galleries to see what an impression the shepherd idea has made on the mind of the artist. Masters of the brush have ever loved to paint Jesus as a shepherd. Wherever that picture is displayed, human eyes are attracted by it and human hearts are ministered unto. The heart of a man is like the heart of a sheep, it beats at the sight of a shepherd.

The shepherd idea has worked its way deep into Christian literature. It has molded, more than we think, not only the language but the thought of the Christian church. Do we not speak of the pastoral epistles? and have we not in every Theological Seminary a Chair of Pastoral Theology? and do we not have at our ordinations pastoral charges? Is not one of the most famous of all recent Encyclicals of the Pope entitled, " The Feeding of the Flock "? The shepherd conception haunts us, clings to us, will not let us go. This is the Lord's doing, and it ought to be marvelous in our eyes. Blessed is the man who ponders its significance and allows it to teach him what it has to tell. We lose something by confining the Anglo-Saxon word " shepherd " to the fields, and shutting up the Latin word " pastor " in the church. We know with our intellect that the two words are synonymous, but we forget it often with our hearts. It would help us to say occasionally, "The Lord is my pastor." It would lift the word "pastor" to higher dignity, and pour into it a more heavenly meaning. It would chasten and strengthen every minister of Christ if now and then he would say to himself, "I am a shepherd. My work is the herding and feeding of sheep." Self-condemnation would come to more than one pastor if his people should begin, some day, to speak of him as "Our shepherd."

There is danger in a time like this that the shepherd conception may become obscured. Just as the shepherd idea was swallowed up in the priest idea, causing a blight to fall upon the church, so a calamity of another sort is sure to overtake us if the shepherd idea is swallowed up in the preacher idea. A Roman Catholic boy intended for the priesthood is always looking forward to the time when he can officiate at the mass. The day on which he celebrates his first mass is a red letter day in his life.

A Catholic boy thinks that the chief work of a minister of Christ is to perform a ceremony—offering up to God a wafer which has become in some inexplicable way the body of God's Son. That false idea demoralizes and darkens the entire Roman Catholic world. The Protestant boy intending to enter the ministry looks forward to the day when he will preach his first sermon. The date of the event is a cardinal day in his calendar. Protestant ministers to the end of their life talk about their first sermon, just as Roman Catholic priests talk to the final sunset about their first mass. Both men are alike in putting the supreme emphasis on a public performance, the one on a ceremony, the other on a discourse. The one makes the altar, the other makes the pulpit, the holy of holies of the Christian church. The one thinks the world is blessed by converting the wafer into the body of Christ, the other that humanity is advanced by his exposition of the life and ideas of Jesus. Both are mistaken.

The New Testament knows neither the altar nor the pulpit. The first elders and bishops were not preachers in our sense of that word, and it was not for generations that the Lord's Supper was converted into the mass. The first permanent officials of the local congregations in the days of the apostles were overseers, superintendents, guides, presbyters, bishops,—in other words, pastors, herders of the sheep. The pastoral idea is deeper than the priest idea, or the preacher idea, and it is also wider. Its contents are richer. Priests and preachers impoverish their lives and curtail their usefulness. when they fail to keep alive in their hearts the shepherd idea.

The pastoral notion is disparaged, not only by many ministers, but also by most of our churches. Our Protestant churches look, first of all, for what they call a preacher, a man who is an expert speaker and who can draw and hold a company of listeners. Who ever heard of a man being called to a church because he was a good shepherd! The popular estimate of pastoral service comes out also in the policy adopted by the church in doing its work. No man can be the pastor of more than a few hundred people, and yet churches roll up their membership sometimes to a thousand, while one man is expected to go on doing all the work of the parish. The result is he can do nothing well. He is a failure as a pastor, and soon or late he breaks down as a preacher. Every city church of a thousand members ought to have a staff of pastors, and each one ought to do the thing he can do the best. We ought to utilize in the ministry men of the most diverse endowments. We impoverish our church life by limiting the ministry practically to men of a single type. Nearly all our city churches are run on the old village plan: one man is supposed to do everything. No wonder they do not cope successfully with city problems. A village church in a city environment is impotent. Men and money are being squandered in a senseless effort to do the impossible. What our city churches need more than all things else is pastors. A city church like a city hospital or a city school is an expensive institution and laymen must be educated to pour their money into it with a generosity hitherto unknown. It is because Christian laymen as a rule do not know the value of pastoral service that most of our city churches are to-day fighting a losing battle.

When at last the membership becomes unwieldy, and the pastor is seen to stagger under his load, and in sheer desperation the church decides to obtain the services of a second worker, who is that second worker likely to be? Some young man, perhaps, just out of the seminary, who is willing to work for his clothes and board, or some aged saint whose waning vitality has closed to him every other door. For the pulpit, everybody is certain that a man must have brains, talent, genius, but for pastoral service it is a common impression that almost any man is sufficient. The churches show

their estimate of pastoral service by the
policy they pursue in securing it.

The Schools of Theology have been in
some measure responsible for the ignorance of the churches. A glance at the cur-
riculum of the old-fashioned seminary is
sufficient to show that pastoral theology was
in the judgment of the doctors a subordinate branch of knowledge. Greek and
Hebrew, comparative religion, the confes-
sions and creeds, sacred rhetoric and elocu-
tion, homiletics in all of its branches, sys-
tems of theology—surely these have had
the uppermost seats at the theological
feasts, and young men have been trained
not to scoff at pastoral work, but to place
it in a subordinate rank. Spiritual ther-
apeutics, casuistry or cases of conscience,
the cure of souls, the remedies provided in
the Christian pharmacopœia, the application of Christian principles to specific ail-
ments of the individual heart, surely these
are studies which have received less than
their deserts. Then again the science of

sociology, the art of coöperation, the philosophy of fellowship, all of those knowl-
edges and disciplines involving social life
and communal action, have been too often
slighted, if not completely ignored.   Many
a seminary graduate floundering amidst the
complicated forces of his first parish has
cried out in humiliation and anger: " Why
did they not teach me in the seminary how
to organize my work and how to grapple
with all this mass of tangled and critical
problems for whose solution I am totally
unprepared!"

One result of this disparagement of pastoral service is visible in the sentiments en-
tertained by many young men entering the
ministry.   They say quite openly that they
despise pastoral work.   Study they enjoy,
books they love, preaching they revel in.
But as for shepherding the sheep, their soul
hates it.   They like to feel that they have
special gifts for the pulpit.   When their
friends prophesy for them a glorious pulpit
career, their heart sings.   The work of the

shepherd was an abomination, we are told, to the ancient Egyptians, and so it is to all pulpit Pharaohs who are interested in building pyramids out of eloquent words. The fear of breaking down in a sermon weighs like a nightmare on them, the fear of breaking down in pastoral duty is never once before their eyes. A slip in the pulpit brings gnawing remorse, a blunder in pastoral work gives the conscience not a twinge. Public worship is to them the be-all and the end-all of ministerial life. They have not read the New Testament sufficiently to observe that public worship is not made the one thing needful either by Jesus or the apostles, and that while it is not to be neglected there are many weightier matters of the law.

In defense of young men who look askance at pastoral work it may be said that youth is the time when the intellect is voracious for ideas, and when God intends men to furnish their mind. Young men are, if intellectually alert, interested more in ideas than in men. Moreover the gift of speech is a gift early developed, and the love of speaking is one of the delights of youth. Shepherding sheep, one at a time, cannot be expected to be so fascinating to young men as blowing a thrilling message through a silver trumpet in the ears of a crowd on the Lord's Day. Moreover, young ministers have the peculiar frailties which are inseparable from youth. They like commendation. They are sensitive to applause. They are fond of the limelight—how can they help it? They are encouraged by attention in the public press. Papers are everywhere, and their contents are discussed in every circle. To get into the papers, therefore, is one way for a minister to multiply his power. And to get into the papers a man must preach. He can say things in the pulpit which the reporters will be glad to print. He can accomplish things from the pulpit which the world needs to have done. Young men are rightfully ambitious to make their lives count for the most possible. They are commendably

eager to gain attention to their message.
The pulpit is a sort of housetop from which
they can shout their tidings to all the town.
In pastoral work a man is on the ground,
and the world is not likely to pay attention to him. Again, youth is naturally impatient. It wants things done, and it wants
them done at once. To deal with men one
at a time is tedious and exhausting. To
coax one bad boy into obedience to his
mother, or to lift one slave of drink into
sobriety and freedom, or to brighten one
humble household with a smile and a prayer—this requires patience and tact and sacrifice, and it seems puttering work compared with making a great hit with a crowd
of people all at once on the Lord's Day.
Youth longs to do things in haste, and for
this we should not be sorry. It is the glory
of a young man that he wants to move fast,
and that he is not so patient with things as
they are, as an old man is. It is a certain
burning swiftness of the blood which makes
many a young man averse to pastoral work.

There are certain gifts and graces which

like the oak mature but slowly. One of these
is sympathy. Sympathy is the outgrowth
of experience. The experience of young
men is limited, and for this they are not
to blame. Many a young man has been
sorely troubled on entering his first parish
because of his feeble love for people. On
examining his heart he has found it cold
and dead. He has looked at the men and
women before him and confessed to himself that for most of them he does not
care. There seems to be no point of contact between him and them. He has been
studying and they have simply been ex-
isting. They know hardly anything, he
knows a lot. He has been thinking, they
do not seem to have thought at all. He is
quite familiar with all the great thinkers of
Germany and of England and Scotland,
but in his parish these kings of modern
thought are quite unknown. The very
wisest of his people do not know what
Ritschlianism is, or Pragmatism, or Vital-
ism, or Monism, or Modernism, or any-

thing else worth the attention of the modern man. The men in his parish are simply buying and selling, working and playing. The women are keeping house and fulfilling various social functions. The world is eating and drinking, marrying and giving in marriage, very much as it did before the flood. How is it possible for a young man reared in the world of books to take a hearty and genuine interest at once in a world so stupid and belated? It is by no means easy for a young man to become a shepherd, and he ought not to be discouraged if he cannot become one in a day, or a year. An orator he can be without difficulty. A reformer he can become at once. In criticism of politics and society he can do a flourishing business the first Sunday. But a shepherd he can become only slowly, and by patiently traveling the way of the cross.

The shepherd's work is a humble work; such it has been from the beginning and such it must be to the end. A man must

come down to do it. A shepherd cannot
shine. He cannot cut a figure. His work
must be done in obscurity. The things
which he does do not make interesting copy.
His work calls for continuous self-efface-
ment. It is a form of service which eats
up a man's life. It makes a man old before his time. Every good shepherd lays
down his life for the sheep. If a man is
dependent on the applause of the crowd, he
ought never to enter the ministry. The
finest things a minister does are done out of
sight, and never get reported. They are
known to himself and one or two others,
and to God. His joy is not that his success
is being talked about on earth, but that his
name is written in heaven. The shepherd
in the Orient had no crowd to admire him.
He lived alone with the sheep and the
stars. His satisfactions were from within.
The messengers of Christ must not expect
bands of music to attend them on their way.
Theirs is humble, unpretentious, and oftentimes unnoticed labor, but if it builds souls

first sermon in Nazareth Jesus accepted the program laid down by Isaiah, and this program was to preach good tidings to the poor and proclaim release to the captives, and recovering the sight to the blind, to set at liberty them that are bruised, and to proclaim the acceptable year of the Lord. Speech and action are combined. The Messiah is both to teach and to do. Luke never loses sight of this twofold work. He tells Theophilus that his gospel is the story of what Jesus began both to do and to teach until the day on which he was received up. He says that to the twelve Jesus gave a twofold work. He called the twelve together and gave them power and authority over all demons and to cure diseases, and he sent them forth to preach the kingdom of God and to heal the sick. The twelve understood that they were to do more than preach. They departed and went throughout the villages preaching the gospel and healing everywhere. In our oldest gospel, Mark, the same distinction is made clear. " He appointed twelve that they might be

with him, and that he might send them
forth to preach and to have authority to
cast out demons." This was the work
which he himself had been doing. He went
into their synagogues throughout all Galilee, "preaching and casting out demons."
Matthew maintains the same distinction.
"Jesus went about all the cities and the
villages teaching in their synagogues and
preaching the gospel of the kingdom, and
healing all manner of diseases, and all manner of sickness." It was when Jesus saw
the multitudes distressed and scattered as
sheep not having a shepherd that "he
called unto him his twelve disciples, and
gave them authority over unclean spirits,
to cast them out, and to heal all manner of
disease and all manner of sickness." In
other words, the twelve were not simply
to proclaim in general phrases a message
for the crowd, they were to preach and
they were to deal with men, one by one,
casting out their evil spirits and healing
their diseases.

If, then, we are the successors of the

apostles, we must have the apostolic spirit
and do the apostles' work. We must shepherd the multitudes which are distressed
and scattered, and bring the life and love
of God by our own spirit-filled personality
into the mind and heart of the individual.
It is only by pastoral work that the world
can be saved.

Without pastoral work the minister himself cannot be saved. If salvation is health,
and health is the kind of life which we find
in Jesus of Nazareth, then how can a minister be in sound health who lacks the shepherd heart, and how can he have peace
and joy if he shirks the shepherd's responsibilities and runs away from the shepherd's crosses? The finest test of the con-
secration of a minister of Christ is not in
his public performances, but in what he
does when the world is not looking. It is
hard for a man to tell when he is preaching, whether he is preaching for himself
or for God. To open up glorious ideas, to
clothe them with language which glows,

and speak them in tones which burn, all
this is so delightful that it is not easy for
the preacher to say just why he likes to do
it. But in the obscurity of pastoral service he has opportunity to ascertain whether
he really loves God and how much he is
willing to do for people simply for Jesus'
sake.

A minister can scamp his pastoral work
and still retain his position as the shepherd
of the flock, but he cannot retain his position in God's kingdom. The unfaithful
shepherd is punished by a penalty auto-
matically inflicted and unescapable. Little
by little his conscience is deadened, the
heart becomes less sensitive, the spiritual
eye loses its keenness, and the culprit, still
outwardly devout and publicly honored, is
pushed slowly but inexorably by the hand
of the Almighty into deeper depths of that
outer darkness prepared for all who are
recreant to their trust. Men shirk pastoral
service not because they are strong, but because they are weak. They have not suffi-

cient strength to bend their life to the life of Christ. It is the weaklings and not the giants who neglect their people. It is the Pagan and not the Christian who shines in public and leaves undone the private duties which belong to him as an ordained steward of the Son of God. When a man says, I hate pastoral work, and do as little of it as I can—if he had ears to hear, he could hear the Spirit saying: "Thou fool!"

A few things are certain. We live in a universe created by a Shepherd God. The Lord is our shepherd. Our world is redeemed by a Shepherd Saviour. Our elder brother is a shepherd. The man whom humanity most needs is a shepherd. Every messenger of Christ is sent to do a shepherd's work. We are to stand at last before a shepherd Judge. God is going to separate the good shepherds from the shepherds who are bad. The questions which every pastor must meet and answer are three: "Did you feed my lambs? Did you tend my sheep? Did you feed my sheep?"

tions there be added the task of systematic pastoral visitation, such as is expected in many Protestant parishes, the rounded whole of a pastor's work is supposed to be set forth. But concerning the utility of this pastoral visitation there is widespread skepticism, and against it there is constant revolt. Who has not heard scornful things said about the foolishness of wasting time in ringing door-bells and filling up the afternoon with a round of social calls which exhaust the minister and add nothing to the spiritual welfare of his people? By some the work of pastoral visitation is counted easy. Preaching, of course, is labor, but pastoral calling is recreation— a sort of ministerial play. To others it is not play, but tribulation—an exhausting drudgery, a cruel infliction visited on helpless ministers, sanctioned by tradition but not included in the plan of God. It is because men do not see clearly what pastoral service really is that such service is often scorned and slighted. A few items of

parochial administration are seized upon
and made the sum total of the pastor's
labor. Anything becomes contemptible if
you whittle it down to a splinter. The
seven functions above referred to are only
minor fractions of a pastor's toil.

Pastoral work does not appeal to a large
and noble mind until it is seen in its en-
tirety, and until the wealth of its opportunity and the manifoldness of its responsibility are clearly apprehended. To find
out the scope of pastoral service, we must
go to the Orient where our shepherd metaphor was born, and ascertain what was in
Palestine a shepherd's work. Jesus was
an oriental. He spoke to orientals. He
thought in the terms familiar to the oriental
mind. He belonged to a nation whose
wealth was largely in sheep, and over the
fields of whose history there came constantly the lowing of cattle and the bleat-
ing of lambs. Some of the greatest of the
Hebrew heroes had been keepers of sheep.
All of the patriarchs, the greatest of the

lawgivers, the sweetest of the poets, and
some of the mightiest of the prophets had
in early life been shepherds. To Hebrew
eyes the work of shepherding had a glory
invisible to our eyes. In Palestine, and in
the countries round about, a shepherd's
work was by no means simple or easy. It
was arduous and manifold. It called into
exercise varied faculties, it gave scope for
the exhibition of the loftiest virtues. It
taxed the higher range of talents and developed the noblest qualities of the soul.
By glancing at the range of the shepherd's
duties we shall be able to comprehend what
pastoral service meant to Jesus, why he
phrased his charge to the chief of the
apostles in the vocabulary of the sheepfold, and how it came to pass that the
title chosen by him for himself was
" Shepherd."

I. The Eastern shepherd was, first of all,
a watchman. He had a watch-tower. It was
his business to keep a wide-open eye, constantly searching the horizon for the pos-

sible approach of foes. He was bound to be circumspect and attentive. Vigilance was a cardinal virtue. An alert wakefulness was for him a necessity. He could not indulge in fits of drowsiness, for the foe was always near. Only by his alertness could the enemy be circumvented. There were many kinds of enemies, all of them terrible, each in a different way. At certain seasons of the year there were floods. Streams became quickly swollen and overflowed their banks. Swift action was necessary in order to escape destruction. There were enemies of a more subtle kind—animals, rapacious and treacherous, lions, bears, hyenas, jackals, wolves. There were enemies in the air, huge birds of prey were always soaring aloft ready to swoop down upon a lamb or kid. And then most dangerous of all were the human birds and beasts of prey—robbers, bandits, men who made a business of robbing sheepfolds and murdering shepherds. That Eastern world was full of perils. It teemed with forces hostile to the shepherd and his flock. When Ezekiel, Jeremiah, Isaiah, and Habakkuk talk about shepherds, they call them watchmen set to warn and save.

The first great pastor of the Christian church, Paul, in his farewell address to the officers of the church in Ephesus, emphasizes the importance of the work of watching. His closing exhortation is "Watch!" He gives these men a reason for his warning. Grievous wolves, he says, are going to enter in among them, not sparing the flock. And moreover from among their own selves men are going to arise, speaking perverse things and drawing away many after them. There are two quarters from which enemies are always to be expected: from the outside and also from the inside, from the world and also from the church. Not only will there be wolves in wolves' clothing but there will also be wolves in sheep's clothing, and against both types of wolf the Christian minister must be ever on his guard. The apostle goes on to re-

lives for which he is to render an account.
Watching, surveying, scanning the horizon,
peering into the darkness of days not yet
born, spying out the interior nature of
forces which are working like insidious and
poisonous leavens, calculating the advent of
storms asleep as yet in the caves of coming
days—all this is pastoral work, work which,
alas, is not always conscientiously per-
formed. Many a minister fails as a pastor
because he is not vigilant. He allows his
church to be torn to pieces because he is
half asleep. He took it for granted that
there were no wolves, no birds of prey, no
robbers, and while he was drowsing the
enemy arrived. False ideas, destructive interpretations, demoralizing teachings came
into his parish, and he never knew it. He
was interested, perhaps, in literary research; he was absorbed in the discussion
contained in the last theological quarterly,
and did not know what his young people
were reading, or what strange ideas had
been lodged in the heads of a group of his
leading members. There are errors which

are as fierce as wolves and pitiless as hyenas, they tear faith and hope and love to pieces and leave churches once prosperous mangled and half dead. Or it may be that new conceptions of God and the world were rising like blazing suns in the firmament of the world of thought, and the minds of the followers of Jesus were agitated and perplexed. Instruction was needed to prepare men to accept changed ideas of the Scriptures, of inspiration, and of authority, and the watchman was looking in the other direction. He was studying the past, he was wedded to the antique, he was a devotee at the altars of the preceding generation. He did not see that the old order was changing, giving way to new. And because he did not know what was going on in the world and in his parish, the faith of noble saints of God was shaken and the peace of many hearts destroyed. Watching is one of the chief forms of pastoral service. A pastor is a watchman. His home is in a tower.

II. A shepherd in the East was also a

guard.   His mission was not only to oversee, it was likewise to protect. He was a guardian of the sheep. He was their defender. Sheep are among the most defenseless of animals. They are not provided with weapons of attack or defense. They can neither bite nor scratch nor kick. They can run, but not so fast as their enemies. A sheep is no match for many an animal half its size. Its helplessness is pitiable. It is dependent absolutely on human strength and wisdom. Its safety lies entirely in man. Man is its refuge, its buckler, its shield, its rock, its fortress. Everything that the Psalmist calls God, a sheep might call its shepherd. The walls of the sheepfold are built by the shepherd. When there are no stones, he builds thorn bushes into barriers. The door of the sheepfold is made by him, opened and closed by him. By his foresight the sheep are protected. By his courage they are saved. He defends them in the hour of attack. He safeguards them

which stain the mind and eat out the bloom
of the heart, all this work of prevention is
pastoral work, and what work is more important and more difficult? To create ob-
structions in the stream of evil, to build up
walls against the packs of animal forces
which lacerate and ruin, to erect safeguards
on the brink of dangerous precipices over
which thousands have fallen to their death,
this is pastoral work, and it is the shame of
the church that not more of it has been done.
We have spent too much time in coaxing
half-dead sheep back to life again, and not
time enough in building barriers against
the wolves. Ministers in large numbers do
not anticipate as they should the perils
which their people are bound to meet.
They do not take the necessary precau-
tions for themselves or for those entrusted
to their keeping. They do not plan and
work for the creation of agencies for warding off attack. They do not intercept by
skillful and timely measures the ruin which
the enemy has plotted. There is demand in

every parish for constructive work of the highest order. No other work demands a loftier grade of intelligence and skill. The losses of the average parish are appalling, and one reason is that life is not properly protected. The shepherd has no genius for constructing sheepfolds which will keep out the wolves. He does not seem to know that it is his duty to devise means and measures for meeting and overcoming the hostile forces which are forever making warfare on the church of Christ. He does not guard.

III. The shepherd is a guide. Sheep are not independent travelers. They must have a human conductor. They cannot go to predetermined places by themselves. They cannot start out in the morning in search of pasture and then come home at evening time. They have apparently no sense of direction. The greenest pasture may be only a few miles away, but the sheep left to themselves cannot find it. What animal is more incapable than a sheep? He real-

izes his impotence, for no animal is more
docile. Where the shepherd leads, the
sheep will go. He knows that the shepherd is a guide and that it is safe to follow
him. The shepherd cannot drive the sheep,
he must lead them. Mules and hogs can
be driven, but not sheep; their nature is to
follow. In the East a deal of guidance is
necessary. The pasture is often in spots
and strips, and sometimes the strips and
spots are far apart. Streams are not abundant, and at certain seasons the land is
parched by drought. In such a country the
work of guidance is difficult and urgent.
The poet who thought of God as a shepherd knew well a shepherd's work. He
thought of God first of all as a leader. God
goes ahead and finds the streams which are
sweet and the pastures which are fragrant.
" He maketh me to lie down in green pastures. He leadeth me beside still waters."
This idea of leadership was in Jesus' mind
when he said: " I am the good shepherd."
His sketch of the Palestinian shepherd was

true to the life. " The sheep hear his voice, and he calleth his own sheep by name and leadeth them out, and the sheep follow him for they know his voice."

It is a commonplace that a minister is a leader, and yet not every minister knows how to lead. In other words, he is not a good pastor. Some ministers try to drive. Their fatal weakness is an inability to see that shepherds cannot drive. Such men are always cutting, lashing, forcing, and therefore always getting into trouble. They are continually quarreling with their people, and for no other reason than that they do not know how to lead. They push and do not draw, they shove and do not woo. They believe in propulsion and not in attraction. They lack the magic of the shepherd touch. They do not know human nature, they do not realize that men, like sheep, must be led. A minister must always go in advance of his people. He must lead them in thought. It is tragic when a minister is not the intellectual leader of his peo-

ple. If his conceptions are the conceptions
of the average man, if his ideas are the safe
and commonplace ideas of the general community, if in his attitude to great reforms
he is not in advance of the crowd, if in
pulling down strongholds of evil, many
are more aggressive than he, he is not a
shepherd. A minister who does not lead is
shirking a capital branch of pastoral work.
His people would follow if he would only
lead them. But he hides himself in the
middle of the flock, and often lags in the
rear. Sometimes he is not a leader even
in parish enterprise. He does not teach his
people how to work. Men and women, no
matter how gifted and well meaning, do
not know how to do Christian work unless
instructed. The work lies in masses all
around them, but they will not take hold
of it unless their hands are trained. The
doors of opportunity stand open, but the
average Christian will not enter unless encouraged. It is surprising how much work
any congregation of Christian people will

accomplish if only they have a leader. A leader is not an exhorter, or a scolder, or a declaimer, but a man who goes ahead and points out the particular things which ought to be accomplished, and not only points them out, but also shows in what manner they may best be done. Some ministers can see a huge work which ought to be attempted, but they cannot lead their people into it. They can describe critically the strategic nature of the battle that ought to be fought, but they never get their people on to the battlefield. They are visionaries, dreamers, but not shepherds. They do not lead. No one is really a leader whom men do not follow.

IV. A shepherd in the East was a physician to the sheep. Sheep, like human beings, have diseases, and like all other living creatures on our planet they are liable to accident and misfortune. They cut themselves, their feet get sore, they break their legs, they fall the victims of distempers and infirmities of many kinds. The ori-

ental shepherd was a healer of the diseases
of his flock. There was usually at least one
of his sheep which was lame and ailing,
and upon this invalid the shepherd be-
stowed more abundant care. The sheep
that had no appetite, the sheep that on a
journey got out of breath, the sheep that
limped and occasionally lay down, these
were the sheep toward which the shepherd's sympathies went out. The nature
of his calling compelled a shepherd to be a
doctor and a nurse.

Jesus the good shepherd always regarded
himself as a physician. He could not understand why his enemies objected to his
paying attention to the sick. When he sent
his disciples out he told them both to preach
and to heal, making it clear that his envoys cannot fulfill their mission by words
alone, they must do a certain work.

It is the mission of the pastor to " minister to minds diseased; to pluck from the
memory a rooted sorrow; to raze out the
written troubles of the brain; and, with

some sweet oblivious antidote, to cleanse
the stuff'd bosom of that perilous stuff,
which weighs upon the heart." There is
always some one ailing in the parish,
not physically only, but mentally, morally,
spiritually. The diseases of the soul are
multitudinous, and the remedies provided by
the Almighty are efficacious only when applied by a skilled practitioner. There are
soul diseases peculiar to certain ages and
certain temperaments, and certain callings
and certain environments, and the minister
ought to know the symptoms of these diseases, the stages of their development, and
the hygienic processes by which they may
be cured. There is loss of appetite, emacia-
tion, debility, fever, blindness, deafness,
palsy, paralysis, diseases of the heart, oc-
cult and baffling distempers of the mind,
depression, prostration, and agonizing par-
oxysms of the spirit. Here is a field in
which the minister is called upon to put
forth his skill and strength. His mission is
to the sick, and all sick people are not sick

and to each of them is given a part to play
in the world's life and work. It is both
Christian humility and common sense for
a minister to work hand in hand with men
who have learned God's laws in other prov-
inces of his vast kingdom and to avail himself of whatever help God is willing to
render through them. While the minister
must not attempt to supplant the physician,
he can never, without loss, however, forget that he himself as pastor is a physician,
and that through all of the agencies which
God places within his reach, it is his duty
to work for the restoration of humanity to
physical as well as to spiritual health.
Often the root of moral diseases is in the
flesh, and many a spiritual phenomenon becomes explicable only by the knowledge of
physiology. The physical health of his
people is always a matter of concern to the
instructed pastor. Whatever ministers to
their physical health will likewise render
possible a fuller unfolding of their spiritual
nature, and a more efficient service in the

kingdom of God. Hygiene, physical, moral, and spiritual, is a part of the work of the shepherd. The shepherd is the physician of the sheep.

V. The shepherd is a savior. He saves sheep that are lost. A critical part of the shepherd's task is rescue work. Sheep have a propensity for getting lost. They lose their way through stupidity and also through heedlessness and folly. A sheep will keep his nose to the ground following the strip of greenest grass, little by little separating himself from his companions, until at last, his companions being completely left out of sight, the poor isolated animal does not know where he is. When once he realizes his lost condition, he is furious to find his fellows. He cannot live alone, he was made for society. When by himself, he is timorous and easily panic-stricken. Every sight alarms him, every sound makes him afraid. He rushes hither and thither seeking his way, but his search is generally fruitless. A lost sheep does

not get home. The more he tries to find
his path, the farther is he likely to be from
the fold. In his desperation he may run
into a thicket or sink into a morass or fall
into a pit and there perish unless the shepherd finds him. A sheep is like a man in
that he cannot save himself; without a
savior he is irretrievably lost. In the Old
Testament the care of the shepherd for his
sheep is finely dwelt on. Prophets and
poets are always extolling the shepherd's
care, but it is not until we pass into the
New Testament that the shepherd's solicitude for the lost sheep becomes paramount
and controlling. In the preaching of Jesus
we get for the first time the full picture of
a shepherd going out to seek the sheep that
is lost. It was of this trait in shepherdhood that Jesus loved to think. This was
the ruling disposition of his own great
heart. When he saw the multitude he was
moved with compassion for them because
they were distressed, and scattered as sheep
not having a shepherd. One of the sayings

this trait of the good shepherd—the disposition to seek the lost—they are interested in the sheep in the fold, the sheep outside do not much concern them. They soliloquize thus: "Why do they not come in? If they are outside it is their own fault. The church is open. The Word of God is preached. The sacraments are administered. This is enough." That is a style of argument that brings relief to a certain type of ministerial mind. Such ministers have few converts. The number of accessions on confession is small, but this does not disturb them, for they do not feel any special call to the straying sheep of the house of Israel. They like sheep who do not stray, they are fond of good sheep who behave well and give the shepherd no trouble by getting lost. It is a great bother to go after a sheep that has broken away— a sacrifice which it is hardly necessary to make. There are other ministers who have a passion for the lost, but only the lost of one particular type, men and women who have never belonged to the church. How to reach the so-called unchurched masses is to these ministers the only great problem. All sorts of devices are adopted to catch them. When any of them are won, that ends the interest of the minister in them. They are now church members, and the work must go forward of rescuing others who are lost. But, alas, many of those who have been found soon wander away. They do not remain saved. They are ignorant and foolish and like sheep stray from the fold, but the minister does not go after them, he likes sheep lost openly and notoriously, but not straying sheep. He feels incensed that his straying members have forsaken him, he takes it as a personal affront, he resents their habit of roving. He may in a fit of petulance say he is glad they are gone. At first they dropped out of the prayer meeting, but he did not go after them, or send any one else after them. They came only occasionally to the Sunday service, and later on they came not at all, but he gave them no admonition. He was nettled by such backsliding, but said nothing. His sermons, he knows, have been up to high-water mark. The Word of God has been faithfully preached. He has never been more faithful in his study, so that there can be no shortcoming in him. If sheep ramble off, it is because of their own folly; if they straggle behind, it is because they are not worth saving. Many a minister comforts himself in this way. The result is that the losses of the church are tremendous. Some churches receive large accessions, but never grow. They are always adding new names, but doing nothing greater for the kingdom of God. Every parish is losing constantly, and part of the loss is inevitable. Christ lost one of his twelve sheep, and no minister is blameworthy because he does not keep all. But much of the loss is culpable. It could be reduced greatly by more faithful shepherding. Straying sheep could in many cases be brought back if only the shepherd would

go after them. Sheep lost for the seventh
time could be recovered if some one in the
parish possessed the patience and ingenuity
of the seeking heart. The losses are usually gradual and consequently unnoted. If
the minister should hear some morning that
twenty-four of his members were never
coming to church again, he would be rightfully alarmed. "Why is this?" he would
say. "What is the matter? What is wrong
with me or the church that all these people
are going away? What sort of wolf or
jackal has gotten loose in my flock, causing
this demoralization?" But if these church
members drop out one at a time silently and
without public notice, one on the average
each month, the minister, if not a shepherd,
will pay no attention to the drain, even
though at the end of two years all the
twenty-four will have gone, and the loss to
the church will be as great as though all
the twenty-four had departed on the same
day. The minister who allows one sheep to
drop out of his flock without a wound in

his heart and without lifting a hand to
bring that sheep back, is not a good shepherd. A good shepherd dog will wheel
round and round the flock, carefully bringing into place every sheep that shows a
disposition to lag behind. His instinct tells
him that the art of shepherding is the art
of taking care of the sheep which is slip-
ping away. He knows in his own brute
way that he brings disgrace on the race of
shepherd dogs unless he can rescue the
sheep that is losing itself. Ought not a
shepherd man to be as wise as a shepherd
dog? A minister may be a good sermon-
izer, he may preside at weddings with
grace, and officiate at funerals with dignity,
but he is not a good pastor if he maintains
an unruffled mind when a solitary member
of his flock wanders away. The work of
watching demands vigilance, the work of
guarding demands prudence, the work of
guiding calls for courage, the work of healing involves skill, but the work of rescuing
is a work of love. Many a minister would

be a better shepherd if he had a more loving heart.

VI. That the feeding of the sheep is an essential duty of the shepherd calling is known even to those who are least familiar with shepherds and their work. Sheep cannot feed themselves, nor water themselves. They must be conducted to the water and the pasture. The water in the Orient is often gotten out of wells, and drawing it is a part of the shepherd's work. The grass varies with the seasons, and the shepherd is ever changing the location of his flock. He shifts it from place to place, keeping it now in the valley and now on the plain, and now leading it to the very mountain top in order that it may be nourished. Everything depends on the proper feeding of the sheep. Unless wisely fed they become emaciated and sick, and the wealth invested in them is squandered. When Ezekiel presents a picture of the bad shepherd, the first stroke of his brush is—" he does not feed the flock." When Jesus hands over the church to Simon Peter, his first word is—" feed." The work of feeding is never to be neglected. That God feeds his people like a shepherd was an idea full of comfort to the Hebrew heart. He prepares the table, he causes the cup to run over, that is a part of his gracious ministry to men. Jesus claims to be the good shepherd, and one of the grounds of his claim is that he feeds. We are to come to him both to drink and to eat. He is the bread of life and also the water of life.

The idea of feeding is woven into the popular conception of the minister's work. " He does not feed his people " is considered to be among the most damning of accusations which can be brought against the pastor of a church. An English poet has sketched in a single line the portrait of a minister who is what a minister ought not to be: " The hungry sheep look up and are not fed."

But while it is universally admitted that the minister must feed his people, it is sur-

prising how little attention is paid by many
a minister to the subject of nutrition, and
how little thought is given to the art of feeding.   Much emphasis has been placed on the
art of sermon writing, how to choose the
text, how to unfold the idea, how to illus-
trate and adorn the truth, and how to perfect the argument.   The world is hardly
able to contain the books which have been
written to tell ministers how to write sermons.   But in many of these books the
idea of feeding is not considered.   The sermon is not looked upon as a form of food
to be adapted to a particular appetite, and
to be made capable of assimilation by a
particular stomach.   The feeding of a congregation is one of the most momentous and
difficult enterprises which any man can un-
dertake.   There is in every church a wide
variety of ages, temperaments, appetites,
tastes, constitutions, and a great variety of
foods prepared in different ways is consequently demanded.   The lambs are to be
fed.   Lambs are of different ages and have

different needs. The sheep are to be fed.
The sheep are of different grades and natures. The problem of problems is how to
feed all these different kinds of lambs and
sheep on food which shall be suitable for
each one. The pastoral instinct is nowhere
more sorely needed than in the work of
preaching. Many would not call preaching
pastoral work at all, but what is it if it is
not pastoral? No part of a minister's work
is more strictly, genuinely pastoral than the
work of preaching. When the minister
goes into the pulpit, he is the shepherd in
the act of feeding, and if every minister
had borne this in mind many a sermon would have been other than it has
been. The curse of the pulpit is the super-
stition that a sermon is a work of art and
not a piece of bread or meat. It is supposed to be a declamation or an oration or
a learned dissertation, something elegant
and fine to be admired and applauded and
talked about by eulogizing saints, or carped
at by stiff-necked, unreasonable sinners.

Sermons rightly understood are primarily
forms of food. They are articles of diet.
They are meals served by the minister for
the sustenance of spiritual life. If this
could be remembered it would help many
a minister to get rid of his stilted English
and to cut off a lot of his rhetorical ruffles,
and to free him from his bombastic elocu-
tion, and to burn up the ornamental intro-
ductions and skyrocket perorations. The
shepherd's work is plain and humble.
What true shepherd ever tried to make a
show? A shepherd has his eyes upon the
sheep, and his first concern is that the sheep
shall have enough to eat. Feeding sheep
is not romantic, the poetic element in it is
not conspicuous. It is not an act which
can be done with a flourish. It is prosaic
but vital work, and is never well done unless it is done by a man who has an honest
and an earnest heart. There are few preachers who preach simply enough. Their
English is too bookish and their style is
too involved. They want to be Demos-

thenes or Cicero and are not content to be
a shepherd. An interesting book could be
written on pastoral preaching, preaching
that individualizes and feeds. How to make
sermons that will pass easily into the blood,
how to unfold Bible texts in a way that will
furnish nutriment to the nerves of feeling
and action, how to offer truth so as to
satisfy the cravings of the human heart and
make it strong in the doing of God's will—
is not that one of the cardinal problems
of the minister? and has it been, do you
think, sufficiently considered? Pastoral
work is not simply making social calls, pastoral work is also preaching. The minister
does not cease to be a pastor when he goes
into the pulpit, he then takes up one of the
shepherd's most exacting and serious tasks.
We sometimes hear it said of a minister:
"He is a good pastor, but he cannot
preach." The sentence is self-contradic-
tory. No man can be a good pastor who
cannot preach, any more than a man can be
a good shepherd and still fail to feed his

flock. A part of shepherding is feeding, and an indispensable part. Some of the finest and most effective of all a minister's pastoral work is done in his sermon. In a sermon he can warn, protect, guide, heal, rescue, and nourish. The shepherd in him comes to lofty stature in the pulpit. It is well then for a minister to ask himself now and then: "Am I a good pastor in the pulpit? Am I keeping the people too long in this particular field because I happen to like the landscape from this standpoint? Am I compelling them to browse too long in one favorite pasture? Have they nibbled every green thing in it down to the earth, and are they hungry now for grass that grows higher up on the mountain? When I preach am I doing a shepherd's work? Am I feeding the lambs, or am I exploiting myself? Am I feeding the sheep, or am I pleasing myself? Am I playing with words, or am I breaking bread? Am I building beautiful periods, or am I drawing water? Am I soaring like an eagle, or am

I satisfying hunger? Am I a hireling
preaching for applause, or am I a herder
and feeder of souls? There is nothing
which will so chasten a minister in his sermonic preparation and so discipline his
style as facing the shepherd idea. Christ
was the great teacher, and just because he
was the great teacher he was also the good
shepherd. A shepherd who is skilled in
his work never fails to feed his flock.

VII. The oriental shepherd did one thing
more—he loved the sheep. He loved them
in a way unknown to occidental shepherds.
His relations to them were closer and more
tender than anything found in the modern
sheep-raising world. The solitude of those
eastern lands created wondrous intimacies
between animal and human life. Man and
beast became linked together by ties beautiful and sacred. There sprang up in the
sheep a fondness for the shepherd, and in
the shepherd an affection for the sheep
which displayed themselves in many ways.
Here is a lovely touch: "He calleth his

own sheep by name." It was not necessary that he should give to each sheep a name, but he did it because he liked them. Love always individualizes. It takes delight in coining pet names. It is not love if it is not personal and intimate. Here is another touch: "He carries the lambs in his bosom." It was not necessary that he do this, but he did it because he liked them. When the shepherd was not watching or guarding or guiding or healing or saving or feeding, he was doing something finer than any of these—he was communing with the sheep, playing with them, talking to them, and entering so far as a man could, into their poor brute life. The result was that the sheep were devoted to the shepherd. They knew his voice, every cadence of it was music, every inflection was an inspiration. The oriental shepherd was a lover of the sheep, and it was because of his attachment to them that in time of danger he thought not of himself but of them. In defending them he was willing to lay down

his life. This was the crowning virtue of
the Palestinian shepherd—his self-sacrificing love.

It is also the crowning excellence of all
the shepherds of Christ's sheep. Paul says
to the Corinthians: "Above all these
things put on love, which is the bond of per-
fectness." Paul is thinking of the soul as
being clothed with the Christian virtues.
Around these various beautiful manifesta-
tions of the Christian spirit must be thrown
the greatest of the virtues—love. Whatever other virtues a shepherd of Christ's
sheep may have, he is poor and naked
without love. He must have many virtues,
but the one that gives vitality to all of
them, and which binds them all together, is
love. He has various works to do, but his
supreme work is loving. If he loves he
will do all the things which shepherds
ought to do. He will watch! When did
love ever have drowsy eyelids? Love can
outrun the longest night. He will guard.
Love shields with jealous care. Love pro-

tects at all hazards. He will guide! Love
has far-seeing eyes. Love detects the pit-
falls and finds safe paths into the land of
peace. He will heal! The hands of love
are gentle. Love binds up wounds. He
will seek and save! Love cannot sleep so
long as the one it loves is on the mountain
in the storm. He will feed! Love is
the great nourisher at life's feast. Love
satisfies.

Would you know then the work of a
shepherd, look at Jesus of Nazareth, that
great shepherd of the sheep who stands
before us forever the perfect pattern of
shepherdhood, the flawless example for all
who are entrusted with the care of souls.
"I am the Good Pastor," he says, "I
watch, I guard, I guide, I heal, I rescue, I
feed. I love from the beginning, and I
love to the end. Follow me!"

III

The Shepherd's Opportunity

You have all heard that the day of the preacher is gone. The printing press has taken away his occupation. He still goes on speaking, but it is to a dwindling congregation, and by and by all the pews will be empty. The decadence of the pulpit is one of the popular themes of our day. The contrast between the modern pulpit pigmy and the pulpit giant of a former age is a subject with which sportive spirits make merry.

And now it is beginning to be whispered that the day of the pastor also is gone. The modern world has no need of a shepherd. The typical pastor of bygone generations is an antiquated figure for whom no room can be found on the stage of our modern world. The ancient custom of catechizing children

from house to house, and calling entire
households together for Bible reading and
prayer, the fatherly offices of counsel and
admonition, and the gracious and intimate
ministry of the spiritual guide—all this is
a fashion which has passed away. The
world has outgrown the need of a shepherd. Education has fitted men to think
and act for themselves. Man is no longer
a sheep. Every man is his own shepherd. Pastoral guidance is an imperti-
nence. Wealth has increased and has
brought with it a new sense of self-con-
fidence and independence which will not
brook interference from an ecclesiastical
official. Men now have many helps which
they did not possess in former days. A
multitude of magazines and books furnish
all the information and stimulus which are
needed. The pastor knows nothing which
it is not possible for the alert layman to
know. He may, like other men, make social calls and chat about things of current
interest, but the old need for pastoral

attention is gone. Whatever guidance is desired will be gotten from leaders who speak in printer's ink. Besides all this, men are living in strenuous days and have no time to be talked to by a pastor. Business is business and cannot be dropped even for a moment in the heat of the day. Multitudes leave home for their work in the early morning and return fagged at evening time. Through a larger part of the day the children are at school, and during the afternoon the women are absorbed in their social functions. There is ordinarily no hour in the day in which a pastor can meet the entire household. There is no eager anticipation, therefore, of the coming of the pastor. He is busy, and so is everybody else, and pastoral service, being largely uncalled for and consequently perfunctory, can be dispensed with without loss. In large cities the difficulties are unusually great. There is no parish system among our Protestant churches and members of each congregation are scattered over wide areas, rendering pastoral visitation so laborious that church members in large numbers cease to demand it of their minister. Moreover, a considerable section of society has become nomadic in its habits. Men and women flit south in the winter and north in the summer and across the Atlantic between times, and occasionally make a tour of the world. Thousands of Christians own summer homes in which they live the larger part of the year. The winter months in the city are so crowded that pastoral attention seems an imposition. Modern civilization has escorted the pastor to the frontier and politely bowed him out.

Such is the conclusion of many, but it is mistaken. The age of the shepherd has just arrived. Never has he been so much needed as now. Never before have there been so many important things for him to do. To be sure he cannot do his work in the old way. The old order ever changes. New occasions teach new duties, and time

makes ancient forms of doing things un-
couth. The pastor of the early days in his
colonial dress is no longer in demand, but
the world awaits a shepherd who can meet
the needs of the present hour. In one sense
the world is always changing, and in another
sense it is evermore the same. Steam
and electricity alter many things, other
things they do not touch. They have not
changed the processes of the growth of a
grain of corn, nor have they modified the
appetites and passions of the human heart.
The soul is now what it has been from the
beginning, and now as always it needs a
shepherd's care. Civilization transforms
the surface, the interior life it leaves un-
touched. Schools and colleges do not make
obsolete a shepherd's work. The young
men now coming from our universities are
as much in need of pastoral guidance as
any men in the world. Thousands of them
are confused in their religious thinking, not
able yet to reconcile the teachings of Christ
with what they have learned from their

homes of the rich and the poor sickness comes and death, and the desolation of bereavement, and the darkness of doubt and despair. Rich men with their hands filled with gold can lose the higher treasures of faith and hope and love, and, though living in fine houses, they can be miserable and poor and blind and naked. It is a great mistake to assume that well-to-do people have no need of a shepherd. The minister is unworthy of his calling who neglects or scorns the rich. It is a popular delusion that pastors are always inclined to devote more time to the rich than to the poor, whereas the fact is that poor people are not nearly so likely to be neglected by the average pastor as the rich. Not so many rich people would have lost their early faith and degenerated into social idlers and conscienceless worldlings, if they had received more continuous and faithful pastoral care. There is no class more neglected in our great cities than the rich. The pastoral work in a rich community is far more

difficult than in a community which is poor.
It was easier for Christ to help a poor man
than a rich man, and that has been the experience of all his ministers. But the rich
men in Christ's day always had his sympathy and attention and to them full offers
of his grace were given. The poorest beg-
gar and the richest publican in Jericho were
alike the recipients of his bounty. Money
is never going to take away the occupation
of the shepherd, nor will the printing press
crowd him out. Instead of books dispensing
with the shepherd's labor, they give him infinitely more to do. It is printed matter
which causes a deal of mischief in our
modern world. Many false prophets have
gone abroad, and they wear books' clothing.
All sorts of wolves and jackals, of serpents
also and birds of prey, are moving through
the world scattering and tearing the sheep.
The literature of unbelief is enormous, and
millions are reading it. Fools and dunces,
ignoramuses and fanatics, knaves and mischief makers of many stripes, are writing

for the daily papers and magazines, and pour forth in books their shallow thoughts and low ideals and pestilential fancies upon the world. Anybody, no matter how stupid in mind and corrupt in heart, can write a book and find a multitude to read it. False notions, half truths, shallow reasonings, wild vagaries, crazy hallucinations, pretentious philosophizings, silly prophecies, and darkening interpretations sweep over the world like a flood. Immature and diseased and ill-informed and half-baked minds utilize the printing press in disseminating schemes and programs, which if adopted would upset the world. Never has there been such need for sound brains and sane thinking. Never has there been so loud a call for shepherds fitted by natural endowment and training to lead men out of the morasses of erroneous opinions into the hill country of Christian truth. One who comes into close touch with individual men is amazed often at the perverted notions and curious misinterpretations of Christianity which sometimes lodge in the heads of apparently intelligent men. Even persons who have attended church services for years sometimes betray the most astonishing ignorance in regard to things one would have supposed they had mastered in childhood. Teaching from the pulpit does not reach in thousands of cases the special need of the individual mind. It is only by talking face to face with one person as Christ talked face to face with Nicodemus, and face to face with the woman at the well, that the root of the difficulty is reached and the darkness is scattered. The printing press has created new kingdoms for the shepherd to conquer.

It is true that the pastoral problem in great cities is peculiarly intricate and baffling, but no one who knows the modern city would deny that the city needs the shepherd. It is here that the crowds make one think of the crowds which reminded Jesus of sheep scattered and without a shepherd. It is the tragedy of the city that such multitudes have no one to care for them. Thousands of young men are there without parents, and with no strong friend to give counsel. Thousands of girls are there without a mother, and with no one to take a mother's place. Thousands of men and women in middle life are there, broken in health and also in hope, who have surrendered the ideals of the early years. The aged are there looking wistfully at the western sky and wondering. Difficult it is indeed to shepherd so great a multitude, but because a task is difficult is no reason why it should be abandoned. After the skeptic has painted the picture of the city situation as black as he can paint it, and has put into it every difficulty and obstacle to pastoral service which his eye has seen or his mind conceived, the true minister of Christ will not be daunted but will plunge at once bold-hearted into pastoral work. It is a work which requires extraordinary wisdom, unfailing patience, plodding fidelity, unfaltering boldness, a genius for hope, abiding faith, and boundless love, but there is none other that is more clearly the work that Christ just now wishes done, and upon the faithful performance of which the future of humanity more manifestly depends. The cities must be saved, and they are to be saved by shepherds.

It must be conceded that a pastor does not have so good a chance to shine as formerly. There was a patriarchal dignity and splendor belonging to the shepherd of the earlier time which can never be reproduced. Our modern shepherd cannot be so conspicuous. He cannot stand upon a pedestal. He cannot be so picturesque, but he can still be useful, and this after all is in Jesus' thought the highest honor within the reach of mortals. The modern shepherd can be leaven. He can be salt. He can be light. He can go about doing good. He can give. He can be the servant of all. He can lay down his life. The God who is building the world of our day has left in it a large and glorious place for the shepherd.

Let us measure the dimensions of the

opportunity for pastoral service which is now presented. Note, first of all, how sorely our churches need it. For the last ten years we have been hearing constantly of failing church attendance, and reduced accessions, and lowered Sunday School membership, not in one quarter but in many quarters of the Christian world. There are those who feel that the church has come to a crisis, and men are asking if Jesus is indeed the one who was expected or whether it is time to begin to look for another. Along with this shrinking of numbers in our churches and Bible Schools and Schools of Theology, there has gone on a continual shortening of the pastorate. Ministers do not stay with their churches as they used to stay. After a year or two or three, both minister and people are too often glad to sever the pastoral relation. The pastor departs for pastures new, a fresh committee is appointed, and the ordeal of finding the ideal man is once more gone through with. Sometimes the minister stays, to the consternation of many hearts. The peace of the parish is not what it ought to be, there is discontent in the heart of the minister and dissatisfaction in the hearts of the people. Never, perhaps, have there been so many restless and fault-finding parishes as within the last dozen years.

Varied efforts have been made to deal with the situation. Different physicians have made divers diagnoses, and the remedies prescribed have been diverse. One man has said: "Let us enrich the service—people do not come to church because the worship is thin and bald—let us borrow miscellaneous bits of ritual and adorn the order of our service: thus will the church make herself attractive to many who have hitherto stayed away." Another has said: "Let us revise our creed. It is too long and too scholastic. Men of our day are offended by doctrines couched in the language of the past. Let us write a shorter creed. Or, since many men are skeptical in regard to what were once called funda-

mentals, let us do away with creeds altogether. Thus will be made a wide-open
door and multitudes will enter." Another
has said: "Let us advertise our services.
Let us tell the town what we are doing.
Advertising is legitimate, let us use the
newspapers and flood the town with invita-
tion cards, let us blazon abroad the fact
that all are welcome. Thus will men know
that things are moving and that the church
is interested in their souls." Still another
has said: "Let us organize the men, let
us band them together in leagues and clubs.
Our men hitherto have done but little, let
us get them interested in missions and in
various forms of church activity, and then
the kingdom of God will come with power."
Another has suggested: "Let us send for
an Evangelist, a man who has a genius for
catching the public ear. What is needed is
a prophet with flaming tongue who can
draw and hold the people, forcing them to
a decision for Christ and the church. Let
us organize mass meetings, with a great

and glorious choir, and by the sheer attractiveness of the program let us compel the unwilling to come in." Another has said: "We can do nothing with our present preacher—he is a good man, but he cannot preach. He means well, but his tongue is tedious. He is not great enough for so exceptional a field. He might do well where the people are less cultured, but for a congregation so critical and fastidious a different type of man is a necessity."

All these six doctors have agreed in this, that the one thing essential is an attraction strong enough to draw men inside of a consecrated building. Their common assumption has been that the work of Christ is really prosperous only when crowds are assembled in his name, and that the supreme problem of the Christian church is how to devise a Sunday service so attractive that people cannot stay away. And so in many a field one or two or more of these six expedients have been tried. The service has been enriched and then made still richer. It has been embroidered, flounced, and tucked. The creed has been whittled down until nothing at all remained. The advertisements have been large and vivid, and printer's ink has flowed in rivers. The men have been organized and reorganized, and drilled in the art of holding dinners at which only expert speakers gave eloquent advice. Evangelists of vast prestige have delivered their stirring message, and then hurried on their flaming way. One minister has been succeeded by another, in the hope that Chrysostom the golden-mouthed might finally appear. But, alas, after all the remedies have been tested the last state of the church has, in many instances, been worse than the first. It is a stiff-necked generation with which the church to-day has to deal, and these promising experimentations seem impotent in bringing it to Christ. Now and then some one has ventured to suggest that the church should go to the people instead of the people coming to the church, and the new idea has been carried out for a month or two with enthusiasm and high hope. The minister has locked up his church and gone into a theater or into a tent or out upon the street corner, bringing his message to all who would hear. In this enterprising mission some of the faithful have accompanied him, glad to prove by the crucifixion of their tastes and inclinations that they were sincerely desirous of doing the work of the Lord. But in spite of all these efforts prosperity has lingered, and churches by the score have felt themselves discomfited and conquered. After a spasm of zeal the old coolness crept in again. There were crowds for a season, and then the old empty pews were as conspicuous as they were at first.

Only here and there has it been recognized that the solution of the problem lies in the shepherd—one who shall go where the sheep are, not with a grand declamation, but with a heart that loves and solaces and heals. He must live with the people, think with their mind, feel with their heart, see with their eyes, hear with their ears, suffer with their spirit. He must bear their griefs and carry their sorrows. He must be wounded for their transgressions and bruised for their iniquities. The chastisement of their peace must be upon him, and with his stripes they must be healed. They all like sheep have gone astray, and he must be willing to have laid on him the iniquity of them all. It is the sacrificial note in the ministry which is too often lacking in these later days. The minister has become too much a man of a book. Like the ancient scribes he is a scholar and sometimes a pedant. When the Good Shepherd appeared in Galilee, the contrast between him and the other shepherds was perceived at once. There was a sympathy in Jesus' tone and a gentleness in his touch which proved at once that he was with the people in their sorrows and upward strivings. The chief trouble with the modern church is that in too many localities it has lost contact with the life of the town. It is out of touch with the souls of men in their present perplexities and needs, and hence it cannot influence them. The impression is abroad that Christianity is a pretty speech, a bit of idealism, a lovely dream, a stanza of poetry, a piece of Sunday acting, something that the preacher can say by rote, and to which the saints can say, "Amen"; and not a sober, serious, week-day life. What the world most wants to-day is shepherding. The world has many comforts, luxuries in abundance; what it lacks is love. Love cannot be satisfactorily expressed to our generation in printer's ink, in evangelistic appeals, in pulpit eloquence, or in doctrinal statements. The expression which the world now demands is the love of the shepherd who takes the lambs in his bosom, who gently leads those who have their young, and who day by day lays down his life for the sheep. A generation ago the word of God was the Bible, to-day the word of God is Jesus and the man who has the spirit of Jesus. A genuine Christian is the only epistle which the world now cares to read. Multitudes care little for worship, less for church polity, still less for creeds, nothing for traditions and ceremonies. Character is everything. Shepherding work is the work for which humanity is crying. The twentieth century is the century of the shepherd.

The shortening of pastorates is due to the fact that the tenderness and sacredness of the old pastoral relation are fading out. The relation of the minister to the parish is now too often that of a platform speaker to an audience, of a reformer to a community, of an engineer to a machine, and not that of a friend to a company of friends. If the minister is simply a Sunday lecturer, he can leave town any day, and no one will be sadder. If he is only a public reformer, he can depart at the end of any week and many persons will be glad. If he is a machinist, expert in managing organizations, his place can easily be filled by another—engineers are abundant. If he is a shepherd, if he knows his sheep by name, and if his sheep know his voice, he cannot pass from one fold to another without a great loneliness and heaviness of spirit, and without deep wounds in the hearts of those he leaves behind him. It is because the shepherd idea is faint and the orator or preacher idea is so largely dominant that churches are able to change ministers with such slight concern, and that ministers can pass from one parish to another with lightness of heart and even rejoicing. If the church of Christ is to be saved, she must be born again into the glory of the shepherd idea.

That a multitude to-day need shepherding cannot be disputed. The present moral and religious situation is too well known to demand description here. It has been photographed again and again and printed in colors, and the pictures have been held before our eyes so that there is no excuse for confused notions as to the present condition of mankind. It is a somber world on which the electric lights of our brilliant civilization fall. When Jesus looked out upon the crowds in Galilee, he at once thought of a neglected flock of sheep. The shepherds of Palestine had not done their duty. The plight of the people was pitiable. Matthew says that Jesus was moved with compassion because the people were like sheep distressed and scattered. The description is graphic. By " distressed " one is to understand—worried, harassed, vexed, tired out, exhausted. In the other word—" scattered "—we have a picture of a lot of sheep thrown down, one or two lying in this place, a few in that place, still another group in a third place. The unity of the flock is broken because of the attacks of enemies, and the lack of a shepherd's care.

What two better words can be found to paint the present situation? Are not multitudes, to-day, distressed in body, mind, and estate? It is an age of reconstruction, reorganization, readjustment. Mighty movements are taking place in the industrial and commercial worlds. Conditions fluctuate, work is unsteady, positions are insecure. Money takes wings and flies away. Even giants are pushed unmercifully to the wall. It is a money-making age, and men are harassed by the care of wealth. Great fortunes bring with them multiplied anxieties, and the sight of colossal wealth breeds in many minds sour envy and fevered discontent. It is an age of machinery. Steel and electricity perform a deal of work, but never have men been more weary and more heavy laden than just now. Multitudes are perplexed in regard to the things of the spirit. It is an age of new ideas, novel interpretations, bold hypotheses, daring innovations. Everything is the object of furious assault. The industry of the printing press by giving voice to the thoughts and imaginings of a multitude of minds has converted the earth into a tower of Babel, and men are living in a welter of confusion. Intellectual difficulties and practical perplexities combine to cause the present distress. What shall I think? What shall I believe? Which way shall I go? What shall I do? What is true? What is right? What is duty?—in this strange, complex, discordant, bewildered twentieth century. Surely the world to-day is calling loud for guidance. The distress of the multitude is a cry in the ears of the church of God for shepherds.

Men are distressed and they are scattered. Irresistible forces have driven them apart. Millions have passed from one country into another. In the city of New York 1,926,900 white men and women were born in foreign lands. Other millions have passed from rural life into cities. The old homes are broken up, the old ties are severed, families are scattered. Industrial forces drive men into separated groups and classes. The wage-earner and the capitalist have never been farther apart. People are classified according to their financial resources. Every city has its elegant avenues

and its grimy slums. Men are segregated
by forces over which they have no control.
There are chasms as deep and bridgeless as
the gulf in the parable of Dives and Laza-
rus. The result is an enormous mass of
suspicion and envy and ill-will. Large sections of society are sour. The disgruntled
are numbered by the tens of thousands. If
hate is murder, then the world to-day is in
a murderous mood. There are quarters in
which the church can do no mighty
works because of these social estrange-
ments. There are other quarters in which
the message of the church is not even
listened to, so stubborn is the prejudice and
so bitter the resentment. What humanity
just now needs is a great host of peace-
makers, men who shall serve as mediators
between hostile classes of society. What is
needed is the persuasive tone, the gentle
approach, the sympathetic touch. It is the
shepherd rather than the herald who is
needed now, not the man who can deliver
eloquent proclamations but the man who

goes about doing good. It is easy to criticise a sermon, it is not so easy to scoff at good-will manifested in lovely ways. The man who tears the creed to shreds will succumb to repeated acts of kindness. Even the skeptic who is fond of saying that all Christians are hypocrites and all preachers hirelings, cannot permanently stand up against the pressure of a loving heart. The impression prevalent in the non-churchgoing world is that ministers are talkers, salaried palaverers paid to say sweet and soothing things for the men who pay their salaries. There is nothing which will break down this prejudice like the self-sacrificing labors of a shepherd. The questions are often discussed—" How can we reach the unchurched masses—how can we gain the wage-earner—how can we win the laboring man?" It is safe to say the orator will not win him, nor will the theologian, nor the doctor of philosophy, nor the connoisseur in literature. He will surrender only to the shepherd.

and schools, is a paradise for religious im-
postors and magicians. This is because of
our worldliness and the practical godless-
ness of large classes of our well-to-do people. The type of man represented in the
New Testament by Simon the Sorcerer has
never become extinct, and in enlightened
America, as in benighted Samaria, whenever Simon (or his wife) appears and gives
out that himself is some great one, many
give heed from the least to the greatest,
saying: "This man is that power of God
which is called great." Every large city
swarms with cults whose devotees are fed
on various philosophical concoctions more
or less tinctured with the Christian flavor.
The wolves are as shrewd as ever, they
fatten on the sheep. Men and women are
as helpless as of old. Unless shepherded
they become "food to all the beasts of the
field." Ezekiel represents God as mourn-
ing over the situation. "My sheep wander
through all the mountains and upon every
high hill. Yea, my sheep were scattered

to many lips. The emphasis of modern thought on heredity and environment as controlling influences on human life, has worked to break down in multitudes the sense of personal accountability. Children are not to blame since they are what they are because of their parents; and their parents are not to blame because they are the products of society. In this way the individual conscience is dulled and the flame of personal responsibility is snuffed out. The talk to-day is about the social problem, the corporate responsibility, the institutional functions. Society looms large and the individual man dwindles. Here is a call for the shepherd. The shepherd has an individualizing eye. He sees the solitary sheep. He cares for the personal need. The good shepherd always says: "I know my own, and my own know me." He calls his own sheep by name. It is an interesting fact that the last sentence which we can trace to the pen of St. John is: "Salute the friends by name." John is the man who came near to the Good Shepherd's heart, and who narrated in his gospel the allegory in which Jesus says that the shepherd calls his own sheep by name; and the last time John speaks to us he tells us not to forget this personal and individualizing touch. All the Apostles are great teachers of individualism. They learned it from the Master. One of the most thrilling chapters in the New Testament is the last chapter of Paul's letter to the Romans. It is a list of names which ought to be read often in our churches. The names mean nothing to us, but they meant everything to the men and women who owned them, and it ought to warm our hearts to think how warm their hearts became when that chapter was read before the congregation. We think of Paul as a matchless theologian; we do not often enough think of him as an ideal pastor. He was a faithful shepherd even unto death. In the Roman prison condemned to die, writing his last letter he closes with a para-

The intensity of competition makes it necessary that all bungling and wasteful methods be gotten rid of. Every part of the business must be brought up to the highest pitch of perfection. Men are looking for results. The machinery must produce as large a product as possible. The ratio between the energy put in and the product gotten out must be improved. Fortune hangs upon this. The continued existence of the business depends upon it. The standards are everywhere going up. What was counted good enough ten years ago is not tolerated now. Every capable business man is demanding a higher grade of efficiency in every department of his business. In agriculture this movement has already worked astonishing results. It was discovered not long ago that farmers have not known how to farm. They were ignorant of the soil and of the way to get large crops. They did not know how to get out of an acre of ground what an acre ought to yield. And so in recent years expert leaders have been bringing the farmers down to the earth, teaching them that it is not the poor weather which is responsible for thin crops so much as the poor methods of working the soil. They have been taught to go below the soil and make war on a host of bugs and worms which have played havoc with the seed. Farmers have learned that it does not pay to plant poor seed. Iowa farmers were in the habit of planting three kernels of corn to a hill, and were satisfied if they could get one healthy stock with one ear of corn weighing eleven and a half ounces. They are satisfied with that no longer. They are increasing the number of stocks and they are adding to the weight of the ear. The yield per acre has been in some cases doubled, trebled, quadrupled, just by the exercise of more thought. Recently there were some twenty boys representing the Boys' Corn Clubs of the United States who met in Washington City as the guests of our Department of Agriculture. One

boy had succeeded in raising on one acre
over fifteen times as many bushels of corn
as is raised by the average farmer. All
over the world men are at work on the
problem how to increase the yield of the
soil. It is now certain that we have never
begun to get out of the soil what the soil
is ready to give, and that all the dismal
prophecies of the population outstripping
the power of the soil to sustain it, are fig-
ments of the ignorant imagination. A wise
man has recently said, " We must get down
to the ground if we want to get the most
out of it." It is equally true that if the
minister would get the most out of the
people he must come down where they are.
The parish is a farm. The average parish
does not yield as much as it should. Men
are rightfully demanding of the church
greater harvests. Considering its numbers, its wealth and its culture, the church
is not measuring up to present-day expecta-
tions. It does not do enough for social
betterment. Ministers, as well as farmers,

the wall of many a parish? The work that
pastors do in these rigorous, exacting days
must be finer and closer, more intelligent
and scientific, more faithful and painstak-
ing, more personal and delicate, than has
been much of the work in the past. Shepherding work—knowing every sheep by
name, giving every sheep a chance to know
the shepherd—this is the direction in which
an awakened church is bound to move.

The other idea, conservation, has risen
to prominence because of the passion for
efficiency. It is because men are severely
practical and demand larger results, that
the thought of waste has become unendur-
able. Economy has become a watchword
among the nations of the earth. How can
we utilize waste products? How can we
bring into service the energy which is now
squandered? How can we husband the
forces which are running to waste? That
is the question which all alert men everywhere are asking. The world's population
is increasing, a deal of work must be done.

feeding and nutrition, health and disease. Human life has been hitherto wasted horribly. Thousands of lives have been sacrificed to the incompetency of government, tens of thousands to the ignorance of individuals. The world is awakening to the value of life. The awful death rate among infants is not according to the will of God. The babies have not been cared for properly, and that is why so many of them have died. It is not God's good pleasure that disease should fill our cemeteries with premature graves. Cities are making war on the death rate. Already it has been reduced amazingly. In great laboratories of research on both sides the sea men are studying food values, and are grading articles of diet according to their energy-producing power. They are mastering the art of warding off disease. Prophylaxis, or the art of preventing disease, has come to the front; and a new class of medicines, the prophylactics, have taken the precedence of all others. The **surgeon's knife**

The modern physician is nothing if not individualistic. Physicians never deal with men in crowds. "One patient at a time"—that is the rule in all hospitals throughout the world. Each patient has his own chart at the head of his bed. The temperature of his blood, the beat of his pulse, the number of his respirations are carefully noted. Each patient has his own diet, his special remedies, and his particular kind of nursing. It is this sleepless vigilance, this jealous guardianship, this minuteness of observation and delicate accuracy of treatment of the individual man which has filled the modern world with miracles, and given the physicians of the body their unparalleled prestige. It is not by spectacular and scenic methods that the death rate of great cities is reduced, but by the loving care of the one baby, the faithful nursing of the one patient who without this care and nursing would have died. The same policy adopted in our parishes would bring equally astonishing results. Under our present

Samaritans are just outside the parish, earthy and heretical, and yet in God's plan Samaria is always a part of the promised land. The shepherds of the Jewish church before Jesus came had allowed all three classes to slip away from them. Multitudes of Jews were mere formalists, lacking the life of the spirit; others had become utterly hopeless in the eyes of the shepherds; while Samaria was counted accursed, her people unfit to associate with, and her very existence a vexation to the pious Hebrew heart. When the Good Shepherd arrived he understood his business. He at once proceeded to make use of all three classes. He sent idlers into the vineyard. He laid hold of the publicans and sinners, one of whom, Matthew, he placed on a throne, and even of Samaria he said: "Lift up your eyes and look at the fields— they are white already unto the harvest." To him who looks upon the world with Jesus' eyes there are no hopeless deserts, no irreclaimable swamps, nor is there any

Samaria which cannot be made a part of
the Holy Land. Jesus was master of the
method for transforming human nature,
and his was the pastoral method. He made
his way into the Sanhedrim through the
soul of one old man. He touched the
hearts of all publicans the day he befriended one of them, and he broke the hard
heart of Samaria simply by being kind to
one Samaritan woman.

It is when we see that the work of the
Christian church is work on the individual,
that no parish, however limited in territory,
seems really small. There is an unimagi-
nable amount of work to be done in every
parish. Young men ought not to feel that
their life is thrown away because they cannot preach great sermons before a crowd.
Get rid of the oratorical conception of the
ministry, and put in its place the pastoral
idea. You ought not to turn your back
upon a parish because it seems dull and
dead. What parish could have been duller,
stupider, and more hopeless than the valley

of the Vosges before Oberlin took hold of it? What parish could have been more irreligious, reprobate, and godless than Kidderminster before Baxter gave his great heart to it? Never believe that there is a parish on the earth, however desolate or demon possessed, that cannot be made to blossom with the flowers of paradise under the summer warmth created by a shepherd's care.

IV

The Shepherd's Temptations

THEY are many. Let us look at but two. These two are singled out because they are the two against which our Lord and two of his Apostles uttered special and repeated warnings, and because the experience of nineteen hundred years has demonstrated that these two are most insidious, most constant, and most fatal. They are the love of gain and the love of power: covetousness and ambition, inordinate desire to possess for personal gratification, and an unlawful love of advancement, prominence, authority. Christian history makes it clear that these are the cardinal sins which ever lie like crouching beasts at the shepherd's door.

Covetousness is often associated in our mind with money, and it seems absurd to

say that one of the two besetting sins of
the minister is an inordinate love of money.
The world is always ready to accuse the
minister of this, probably because the average man is himself so susceptible to the
alluring power of gold. One of the tra-
ditional taunts hurled at the minister is—
" the bigger the salary the louder the call."
A layman, no matter how great a saint,
may exchange one position for another, if
by so doing he increases his income without
the sacrifice of important interests, but this
in a minister is by many people counted
reprehensible, even positively disgraceful.
There is in many quarters a jealous solicitude lest ministers get more money than
they ought to have, and think more highly
of their salary than they ought to think.

But this accusation is not justified. Ministers, as a rule, are not abnormally fond
of money. No other set of men in all the
world think so little about it, or care so
little for it. That a man is in the ministry
is presumptive evidence that he does not

worship the golden calf. What a dunce a
man would be to go into the ministry for
the sake of making money. Is not the
average minister's salary pitifully small,
and are not thousands of salaries a disgrace to the church? Every man who goes
into the ministry takes, in reality, the vow
of poverty. He turns his back on all the
avenues which lead to wealth. He sur-
renders all hope of ever becoming a rich
man. No man in this country has ever
become rich in money by his service as a
minister. Occasionally a minister comes
into possession of wealth, but it is not
through his salary as a pastor of a church.
There is only the smallest fraction of ministers whose salaries are large, and these
few are large to meet the extravagant ex-
pensiveness of living in great cities. When,
therefore, the critics accuse ministers of
having an itching palm, they deal in cal-
umny. That in this money-loving, money-
seeking, money-crazy country a multitude
of young men are every year turning their

backs on the glittering financial inducements held out by other callings and dedicating themselves to a profession which dooms them to be poor, is one of the sublimest phenomena of our century, and an indisputable proof that the spirit of God is still among us.

But covetousness does not necessarily mean love of money. It is an excessive desire for anything which gratifies one's own cravings. It is the disposition for having and for getting. Money is not the only thing which can be had or gotten, and the very fact that money is shut out from the possible acquisitions of the minister, possibly makes him more covetous for those things which do lie within his reach. Covetousness is a part of our unregenerate human nature, and if it cannot exert itself in one direction it endeavors to make conquests in another. When one speaks of the salary of the minister, he should not stop with the sum of money which the minister annually receives. Money is only

meets one of his two most dangerous temptations. He is tempted to make himself the center of the parish, and like a mediæval Baron exact illicit tribute from the people. A Puritan preacher once declared that " a covetous person lives as if the world were made altogether for him, and not he for the world." Are there no ministers who, according to this definition, are covetous? Do they not often think and act as though the parish were made for them? Men sometimes come out of the seminary with no conception of Christian servantship, no idea that the church is to be first always, no notion that the church does not exist for the pastor but that the pastor exists for the church. There is nothing more dismaying than the tone of the talk in which some ministers indulge. They confess quite blandly that they are looking for a church that will pay them a living salary while they carry out a cherished plan. The church they are looking for must be in a certain locality, must pay a certain salary, must have a certain kind of parsonage, and must be made up of a certain type of people. Sometimes ministers speak of their personal schemes, unabashed and without a blush, and go into their first parish with no other thought uppermost in their mind but that of their own personal advantage. When such a man gets a church, the tragedy begins. He lays out a line of study according to his own taste. He delves in fields to which his intellectual proclivities carry him. He finishes certain investigations, perhaps, which were begun in the school. He gives himself to sundry branches of philosophy or science for which he has a liking. As for the people, who are they? They ought to be satisfied with anything. Every sermon has something in it, and it is the business of laymen to find what that something is. Sunday after Sunday the hungry sheep look up and are not fed. The minister is working, perhaps, for a postgraduate degree; he is, possibly, laying up material for a coming book. He is a greedy, selfish man, and his people droop and die. The physician has come. The patients are before him, but he does not study their diseases. He is experimenting in the laboratory with some new serums and cultures. The sheep are waiting to be guided and fed, but he fleeces them simply to clothe himself. If his conscience is thoroughly dead, he uses the church solely as a base of supplies. He goes into the lecture business, or some other form of remunerative occupation, allowing his people to pay him for work which he does not do. While he is building up his fame and fortune, souls whom God has entrusted to his guidance are left to the mercy of the wolves, and noble causes which might by his leadership be carried to their coronation are permitted to languish and fail. A church going to pieces through sheer neglect while its appointed leader is dabbling in outside ventures is a spectacle which brings pain to the heart of every true lover of God, and must cause anguish among the angels in heaven. Sometimes the church is used simply as a stepping-stone to something better. A minister goes into a parish with no desire to extend Christ's kingdom there, but solely for the purpose of stepping at the earliest opportunity from that parish into one more nearly level with his deserts. Such men are, as a rule, egregiously conceited. Covetousness is a soil in which all sorts of briers and brambles grow. If the poison of covetousness flows in a man's blood, there is no limit to the foolish things he will think and do. By brooding on himself, he generates an abnormal estimate of his worth. Nothing is too good for him. He thinks the highest pulpit in the land hardly worthy of him. He is always aspiring to churches forever beyond him. He thinks he is going to be called by committees who have never once thought of him, and never will. His dreams are pitiable and also disgusting. This is one of the elements in the awful retribution which God inflicts on those who profess to follow in the steps of Jesus, and who are really living solely for themselves. Throughout the country there are, here and there, sour and disgruntled ministers, their hearts in constant ferment, all because they have been denied that recognition which in their opinion their shining merits indisputably deserve. They speak with scorn of " favored brethren " who without half their intellectual resources, and with only a fraction of their merit, have by means of influential friends or chance, or possibly the devil, succeeded in outstripping them. " Put to death covetousness," says the apostle Paul, " it is idolatry." The idolatry of self always leads to hell, and never so swiftly as when the sinner is a minister.

Covetousness leads to conceit, and also to vanity. Every human being has in his heart a peacock, and the peacock is ever hungering after crumbs. The covetous man feeds the peacock in him all the time. People praise his sermons, and this praise makes him voracious for more praise.

carelessness. A man who thinks too much about himself has not sufficient time to give thought to others. Self is a big subject, and when one goes into it, there is no getting through with it. The covetous man is sure to become neglectful of those forms of work which are distinctively pastoral. Ministering in the homes of the sick and the poor, work that involves quiet and obscure labor which no one but God sees, it is here that the covetous minister shows what manner of man he is. There are many duties which a minister cannot escape. No matter how covetous he may be, he will attend to these, for these make for his advantage. He cannot stay away from a wedding, or absent himself from a funeral, or remain at home from a prayer meeting, or go off on a visit over Sunday. Public duties hold him as in a vise. The worst of men will do things which are for their profit, but it is in the doing or not doing of private duties that a minister's true self is disclosed. If he be selfish, he need not go to-day to call on the woman who is ill, he can go to-morrow. The world will not know. If she dies to-night, she will never tell that he did not come. He need not go out of his way to comfort a man who lost his only son last month. An omission of that sort never gets into the papers. The outsider living without hope and without God in the world has no open claim on him, and the claim of the last magazine is imperious, and therefore he can give time to the magazine to the neglect of the outsider. Looking up a member of his church who has grown negligent is not so congenial a task as many another. The wandering sheep does not want to be looked after. Why pester him with pastoral attention? The town will go on just the same with one sheep less in the fold. A bad boy who is breaking his mother's heart needs a bit of admonition, but if he does not get it, he will not divulge the pastor's neglect. A hundred little things ought to be attended to, but every little

thing eats up energy and time, and even
though these little things are really important things in the lives of human beings,
they are matters that can be omitted without the minister being called to account.
It makes a vast difference in the tone and
trend of parish life whether the minister is
faithful in that which is little, or whether
he devotes himself solely to the things
which are conspicuous and big. A considerable part of pastoral work can be
slighted without the lightning falling. Many
of the finest and most critical things can
be neglected without bringing the minister
to open shame; but when a pastor allows
things to run at loose ends in his parish,
and is careless in his response to obscure
but vital needs, he may win golden opinions from many sorts of people, but he
rests under the condemnation of the Good
Shepherd.

Covetousness also manifests itself often
in cowardice. A covetous man, as a rule,
runs at the sight of a wolf. A man careful

of himself has no fondness for danger. He will save himself, whosoever else may be lost. A crisis arises in the parish and he hands in his resignation. Enemies of the flock have appeared, and in the hour when the people most need guidance, the leader abdicates his position. A great moral question is at issue, but he is afraid to come out boldly for the truth and the right. When skies were blue he seemed brave enough, but when the storm burst he was the first to seek cover. In days of peace he blew a furious blast calling the cohorts to battle, but when the enemy appeared he slunk ignominiously from the field. This was because he was a covetous man. He was abnormally fond of his own skin. Covetousness is one of the most subtle and deceitful of all sins. One does not know how covetous he is until tested. The finest test of covetousness is the open mouth of the wolf. In the flash of the fire of a wolf's eyes a man's soul is startlingly revealed. The man with a covetous heart is everywhere and always a coward. When he sees the wolf coming, he flees.

It would be impossible to paint with colors too black the enormity of the sin of covetousness in the envoys of the Son of God. Nothing is so destructive of the Christian faith as a selfish minister. There are laymen whose faith has been destroyed forever by the unworthiness of their pastor. They once had confidence high and glad in Christian ministers, and were foremost workers in the church, and then, alas, one day there came a minister who, preaching with his lips the gospel of unselfishness, hid behind his preaching the rank corruption of an avaricious spirit. Little by little it became revealed that the minister was working for himself, that the welfare of the parish was not in all his thoughts. And when the crisis came he sacrificed the parish to secure his own advancement. When laymen have at their head a covetous leader, they oftentimes say nothing—they sicken spiritually and die. They lose their faith in their minister, and then their faith in all ministers. They lose their interest in their church, and finally in all churches. Woe to the minister who by his selfish heart not only loses heaven himself but closes the door so that others cannot enter—he is the worst man in the parish, he is worse than a robber. A robber may wrong his victim, and still retain a certain sense of honor. Robbery may be his business, and with open face he may acknowledge his unwillingness to be an honest man. But a minister who lives for self is not only a robber but a sneak. He pretends to live for others, and if under his pretense he lives solely for himself, he is the most despicable of all extant rascals. He is the steward of heavenly treasures, and if he looks out mainly for himself, he is recreant to the highest trust which God commits to men. He is a leading citizen of the heavenly Jerusalem, and if at the expense of others he works for his personal aggrandizement, he is a traitor to the kingdom of God.

He is also a blasphemer. He blasphemes

himself, and he causes others to blaspheme.
He becomes the thing which the Son of
God abhorred with all the intensity of his
infinitely pure and honest heart, a hypocrite—a wolf in sheep's clothing.

Jesus has a name for the covetous
preacher. He calls him a hireling. "A
hireling," he says, "is not a shepherd at
all." He lacks the shepherd's heart, and
he cannot do the shepherd's work. A hireling is a man who works exclusively for pay,
his eyes are ever on his wages, his deep-
est motive is gain. He is always counting
up his profits. His god is self. It is amazing how the breath of Jesus has glorified
certain words forever. "Servant," for in-
stance, has never been the same since Jesus
spoke it, nor has "love." He gave some
words a luster which will outlast the stars.
Other words, however, he tarnished, and
left them to make their way down the
centuries disgraced and branded. One
such word is "hypocrite," another is "hireling." One cannot speak the word "hire-

crawled into the garden of the Lord, and was working havoc in the hearts of the Lord's anointed. It is equally striking that Paul in his pastoral address to the elders of Ephesus should say this: "I coveted no man's silver or gold or apparel. Ye well know that these hands ministered unto my necessities, and to them that were with me. In all things I gave you an example, that so laboring ye ought to help the weak, and to remember the words of the Lord Jesus, that he himself said, It is more blessed to give than to receive." In his first letter to Timothy, Paul lays it down as one of the essential qualifications of a bishop, or shepherd, that he shall be no lover of money. By money we are to understand every earthly thing which men count a treasure. There were in apostolic days no comfortable parsonages, no delightful studies, no richly filled bookshelves, no ministerial discounts, no famous pulpits, no eulogizing organizations, no fawning society, no applauding world. Ministers were reviled,

if ministers of the gospel had no ambition. The love of prominence, the craving for distinction, the desire for exalted rank, these are deep-seated instincts in our human nature, and a course of study in theology does not eliminate them. Like all the native appetites of the soul they may become abnormal, bringing to their victims suffering and death. No other sin has wrought such havoc among the ministers of Christ as the inordinate love of place and power. What is the story of a thousand years of church history but the tragic narrative of how the ministers of Christ, little by little, compacted themselves into a hierarchy which became at last the most blighting and intolerable despotism that the world has ever known? The tyranny of the mediæval church was the tyranny of clergymen. Laymen were crowded out of the place appointed them by the church's founder. Reduced to mere spectators, they had no voice whatever in the government of the church, all authority be-

ing gathered up into the hands of ecclesias-
tics, who, rising rank above rank, formed
a compact organization culminating in one
supreme head who claimed authority trans-
cending that of the mightiest of the Cæsars,
and whose agents, distributed throughout
the world, lorded it over the consciences of
men, gathering into their clutches all the
kingdoms of life. It is the supreme tragedy
of Christian history that this ecclesiastical
passion for power in the mediæval church
brought a disgrace upon the cause of Christ
from which it will not recover for another
thousand years. The whole world suffers
to-day because of what mediæval clergymen did. The cause of Christ is hampered
everywhere because of the prejudice plant-
ed in the human heart by the imperious and
high-handed policy of the ambitious leaders of the Church of Rome. The stories of
that tyranny are the property of all mankind. Wherever the name of Jesus is
preached, the enemies of Jesus unroll the
record of the ambition and cruelty and

believe in the priesthood of believers, in the brotherhood of the Lord's disciples. We recognize the danger of church hierarchies, we are on our guard against every increase of ecclesiastical authority, we know that the minister of Christ, if dominated by theories of priestcraft, is the most dangerous enemy which humanity has to face. And yet while thus open-eyed to historic facts and teachings, we may be blind to the evil forces working in our own hearts. Self-assertion, lordly pretension, autocratic temper are not confined to any one branch of the Christian church. Protestantism has not escaped entirely the despotism and the ways of Rome. The old virus still runs in human blood, and to-day, as always, the old injunction is timely: "If any man thinks he stands, let him take heed." We cannot play the monarch in the splendid and dashing way of the mediæval bishop, but it is possible for a Protestant minister to be as insolent as the lordliest of Cardinals, and as despotic as the most tyrannical of Popes. If one were to go up and down our Protestant world, noting carefully the sins of clergymen, would he not write down in his list such as these: autocratic manner, imperious temper, consequential air, dictatorial disposition, self-assertion, hankering after distinction, ambition for higher place, arrogant presumption, refined but earthy lordliness? Every man has in him the elements out of which Rome built a despotism which enslaved the world.

It is worth noting how many things conspire to develop in the minister a proud and imperious disposition. His relation to Christ the Son of God, the consciousness that he is the ambassador of the King of kings, tends to give him a sense of dignity which may easily pass into a vice. The fact that he is entrusted with the oracles of God, and is ordained to minister in holy things, separates him from men engaged in secular occupations, and this, if dwelt on, has a tendency to beget the feeling, " I

am holier than thou." One wonders, sometimes, how much the shepherd metaphor
may be to blame for the exaggerated notions of ministerial prerogative. A metaphor, like every other good thing, is always dangerous. It may be carried too
far. The shepherd idea, if rightly used, is
illuminating, but if abused it is false and
dangerous. It can be construed in such a
way as to imply that laymen are weak and
silly creatures, while clergymen are wonderful beings endowed with supernatural
powers, enjoying unique and exclusive fa-
vors from heaven. Never did Jesus use
the word " sheep " in a depreciatory or dis-
paraging sense. He called little children
" lambs " because lamb is a love name for
a child. He called grown people " sheep "
because the word was dear to Hebrew ears,
and his countrymen had been singing for
centuries: "We are his people, and the
sheep of his pasture." Literally speaking,
men are not sheep at all. They do not belong to an order of creation lower than that

to which the shepherd belongs. The life of pastor and people is on the same level. There is no gulf between the minister and his flock. Pastor and people are members of the same family. They have the same natures and the same privileges. All alike have free access to the throne of grace, all alike are redeemed by the Son of God, all alike are heirs of immortality. It is possible, however, for ministers so to use the shepherd metaphor as to exalt themselves at the expense of the laity, and to set up pretensions which are expressly ruled out by the Good Shepherd.

Whatever the influence of the shepherd metaphor may have been, there is no doubt the nature of the preacher's work has a tendency to feed his love of rulership and to quicken his appetite for absolute dominion. What liberty a minister enjoys in the disposition of his time! No other man but the retired millionaire is such a monarch of his day as is the minister. He can read on Monday morning, or write, or walk, or mingle all three, just as he deems best. On Tuesday morning he can attend to his correspondence, or catalogue his library, or eat the heart out of some new book, or meet a company of friends, just as he decides. The order of his going out and coming in is largely at his own discretion. Within wide limits he is the monarch of all the hours he surveys. Such liberty is dangerous, it has spoiled its thousands. His dominion over his sermons is still more wonderful. He is free to say what the text shall be, the topic, the illustrations, the arguments, the conclusion, and no one can interfere. He can adopt any style of preaching that he likes, he can follow whatever line of thought he chooses. A merchant has to give his customers what they ask for, a hotel-keeper must supply what his guests desire, but a preacher can give what he thinks his hearers ought to want and ought to have, no matter what their needs and wishes really are. For half an hour or more every Sunday morning everything is silent while he speaks. This unparalleled immunity from the noises and interruptions and contradictions which other men are subject to, begets in certain types of men a tone of mind which says: "I am Sir Oracle, and when I ope my lips, let no dog bark." In social life a minister is ever at the front. He is the observed of all observers. Wherever he sits is the head of the table. He has his critics and detractors, but they are not visible at social functions. In social life, especially in small towns, there is a deference paid to ministers which no other man receives. This burning of incense before the minister has a tendency, in many cases, to turn his head, and to lead him to think more highly of himself than he ought to think. Is there a celebration in the town, the minister must attend it; is the fitting word to be spoken on a state occasion, the minister must speak it. Here is a true description of ministers not a few: " They love the chief places at feasts and the chief seats in the synagogues, and the

salutations in the market-places, and to be
called of men, Rabbi." They love these
things because they are human and because
they are accustomed to them, and because
they think they have a right to them. Constant deference and obedience have a tendency to beget in men of a certain grade a
haughty and unlovely disposition.

But mightiest of all the forces working
for the undoing of the minister's heart is
the liberty he has in devising and shaping
the policy of the church. Laymen, as a
rule, are too busy to take continued interest
in church affairs. The result is that in
many parishes almost everything is rolled
upon the pastor's shoulders. Is a change
to be made, he must make it; is a new work
to be undertaken, he must start it; is there
a fresh responsibility to be assumed, the
pastor must shoulder it. In a multitude of
parishes the minister must not only preach
and conduct the prayer meeting, and make
all the pastoral calls, but he must also su-
perintend the Sunday School, manage the

finances, map out the work of every organization, and possibly act even as leader of the singing. No wonder that ministers come to feel sometimes that they are of considerable importance. It was in this way that church government blossomed into Romanism. The laity in the early Christian centuries were largely ignorant, incompetent, and indifferent, and the whole shaping and managing of the church fell inevitably into the hands of its clerical officials. Laymen in our day are not ignorant or incompetent, but many of them are indifferent because they are so busy. They have no time to bother with church affairs. Church administration is left, therefore, largely in the hands of the pastor. This is bad for him, and it is bad also for the church. It makes it easier for the minister to build up in himself a dictatorial disposition and to nourish in his heart the love of autocratic power.

Note some of the ways in which this lordliness of temper shows itself. It is

great sermon," it falls short of the ideal. When men listened to Demosthenes they did not go off saying, " That was a great oration." They said, " Let us march against Philip." There are preachers who by the expression of their face, the poise of their body, and the character of their gestures say quite plainly: " This is God's truth! Do not dare to deny it! Take it! Take the whole of it! Take it immediately!! By the Eternal, I will make you take it!!!" It is not necessary to put grass into the sheep's mouth. Cram the grass down the sheep's throat, and the animal is so flustered he will not eat at all. Put the grass within reach of the sheep, and he will eat it himself. So it is with truth. Hold it up so that people can plainly see it; bring it within comfortable reach of them; give them time to get at it; and they will eat it. Charles Lamb used to say that " the truth of a poem ought to slide into the mind of the reader while the reader is imagining no such thing." The truth of the sermon ought to glide into the mind of the hearer without the hearer really knowing what is going on. It is not an encouraging sign when men go away saying, "What a tremendous fellow that is! What a mighty effort that was!" It is better when they think nothing of the preacher, but go away with a heart disquieted by the memory of things they have done amiss, and teased by the haunting image of a bright ideal; a heavenly perfume hanging round their spirit as sweet as that which filled the room in which Mary broke the alabaster cruse upon the Master's head. Dictators are out of place in the pulpit. Dictatorship is a form of carnal striving after power.

This ecclesiastical lordliness shows itself sometimes in the tone of condescension with which opponents are dealt with, and the haughty insolence with which skeptics are brushed aside. The supercilious and scornful ease with which unbelieving philosophers and materialistic scientists are attacked and overwhelmed by young men, and old men too, in the pulpit, is a sad exhibition of an unchristian spirit. The fact that these opponents of the Christian faith cannot be present to make reply, lays upon the minister an extra responsibility to be scrupulously fair in all his quotations, and beautifully just in all his judgments. To rush furiously upon the ideas of a famous and learned man who is hundreds of miles away and hold these ideas up to coarse and flippant ridicule when the man can neither explain nor defend himself, is not the action of a gentleman.

It is the same spirit which exhibits itself in the vociferous defense of orthodoxy. Every minister is of course under bonds to proclaim and defend what he conceives to be the truth, but he is also under bonds to proclaim the truth in love. If he struts like a rooster and exalts himself like a braggart he may deceive the ignorant into thinking that he is a defender of the faith, but all who have discerning eyes know that he has surrendered it. No man is doing

the cause of truth. All who will not carry out his wishes have the mark of the beast. He is irritated by the least opposition. He is mortified by the failure of a single plan. Any independence of thought he considers a personal affront. If a household refuses to receive him, he calls down fire from heaven upon it. Strong in a clear conscience, he proceeds to break down opposition by the force of his ingenuity. He schemes to get ahead of the insurgents by adroit management. He succeeds—but success can be bought at too heavy a price. The price is always too heavy when success is bought at the expense of the highest Christian spirit in the heart of the shepherd. Many a minister has in the church meeting made a great triumph, only to discover the next day that he was overthrown. A majority of votes were secured for his project, but that amounted to nothing because of the number of hearts which were estranged. A minister may carry his measure, and at the same time lose his cause.

What cannot be secured by sweet persuasion had better be gone without. It is only a bully who tries to tyrannize or club people into advocating his projects, and the minister who attempts it is a man whose heart has been eaten out by the overweening love of power. It is a good thing for a minister to be defeated now and then in order to find out that he is not invincible, and that there are other people in the world besides himself. Victory is often only by way of the cross. A good shepherd ought not to shrink from an occasional crucifixion.

A little Protestant despot, a petty parochial pope, is a sorry caricature of a minister of Jesus Christ. A minister who boasts under his breath that he proposes to run things and who chuckles at his adeptness in manipulating people, and who says by his manner that he is the boss of the parish, is a man who is a stumbling-block in the way of Christian progress. If to the minister the people are only silly sheep, fit for nothing but to be shorn now and then, he is certain to put on airs and bring the Christian ministry into disrepute. He will scold in the prayer-meeting, play the part of a dictator on Sunday, move with a patronizing air among the poor and a supercilious smirk among the rich, give orders in a loud voice to all the officials in the town, while wise men blush for his folly and the church mourns the loss of a leader who because he has not the spirit of Christ no longer belongs to the Master he ostentatiously professes to serve.

The pastor is possessor of a power that is extraordinary and hence he must be evermore on his guard against the temptation to play the lord. Peter in writing to the pastors in his day said: " Tend the flock of God, not as lording it over the charge allotted to you, but making yourselves ensamples to the flock." In other words— your power is not denied, no man can take it from you. It is given you by God himself. Be careful how you use it. Do not strut. Do not clothe yourself in pomp. Do not play the tyrant in your sacred robes. Exert your power in the ways that the Lord has appointed. Exercise dominion after the Lord's own fashion. Be a pattern man after which men can shape their lives. Be a model toward which the people can ever look. Be an example through which the power of Christ can reach and transform the hearts of men. This is the charge given by the leader of the Twelve, and he got his instructions from the Chief Shepherd.

In the training of the Apostles there was no virtue so often extolled and insisted on as humility. The Twelve were intensely human, and under the influence of Jesus' personality and ideas, new ambitions awakened in them, and they began to dream of lofty places which they were going to fill in the coming kingdom. It is one of the mysteries of sin that men can have their minds filled with thoughts of self-abnegation and unselfishness and at the same time be dreaming of preëminence and power. The men who were with Jesus at Cæsarea Philippi and heard his words about the coming tragedy of the cross, began immediately to discuss the old, fascinating and tormenting question, which one of them was to be the greatest. They were not sinners above all others, we are men of like nature with them. We too can listen to the words of Jesus about humility and self-renunciation, and repeat them to our people, and at the same time nurse in our hearts ambitions to climb and shine and dominate.

There are certain passages in the gospels especially appropriate for ministers, paragraphs which ought to be read again and again in the inner chamber when the door is shut. One of them is the eighteenth chapter of Matthew's gospel, with its story of Jesus summoning the Twelve and taking a little child and setting him in their midst, and saying: "Except ye be converted, and become as little children, ye shall not enter into the kingdom of heaven. Whosoever, therefore, shall humble himself as this little child, the same is greatest in the kingdom of heaven." The simplicity and unpretentiousness of an unspoiled child is a revelation of what Christ expects in his ministers. A second classic passage is Matthew, the twenty-third chapter. " Be not ye called Rabbi: for one is your teacher and all ye are brethren. Call no man your father on the earth: for one is your father, even he who is in heaven. Neither be ye called masters: for one is your master, even the Christ. He that is greatest among you shall be your servant. Whosoever shall exalt himself shall be humbled: and whosoever shall humble himself shall be exalted." There is a danger lurking in titles. The word which Rome selected for her priests has had much to do with perpetuating her error and riveting her power. It is not good for ministers to be called by their people " Father." It is not good for the ministers themselves. It assumes a dignity and prerogative in the minister which do not exist, and an imma-

turity and dependence in the people which
are not normal or wholesome. Ministers
are not teachers in the sense in which Christ
is a teacher. They are not masters in the
way in which Christ is a Master. They
are his representatives, but they do not take
his place, nor possess his power. There is
but one Lord, Jesus Christ, God's Son. A
third chapter for pastors is the thirteenth
chapter of the gospel of St. John. The
tragedy in the upper chamber is one of the
darkest in human history. The twelve men
who have spent years in the close compan-
ionship of the most unselfish man who ever
lived, enjoying the illumination of his
teaching and the cleansing power of his
prayers, are still so petty and so selfish at
the very end of their Master's life that they
cannot sit down to partake of a farewell
dinner without childish squabbling over the
order of their places at the table. It was
when their hearts were feverish and resent-
ful that Jesus took the basin and the towel
and proceeded to wash the disciples' feet.

After the work was completed he said: " Ye call me Teacher and Lord: and ye say well; for so I am. I have given you an example that you also should do as I have done to you. If ye know these things, blessed are ye if ye do them. " From the upper room Jesus went to the garden of Gethsemane, and from Gethsemane to the cross. It made men laugh to see a king crucified. They had never seen a king without a plume and without a crown. He was crucified, but King he was, and is, and shall be forever. From his cross he rules the world.

In his hands he holds all souls. His claim upon no one of them has ever been relinquished. He is the shepherd, and all the sheep are his. The minister speaks of his church, his people, his parish—and this is proper if he understands the meaning of his words. As distinguished from one another, one parish belongs to one man, and another parish belongs to another man, but in the deep sense all parishes alike belong

to Christ. The human shepherds come and
go in a continuous procession. A minister
arrives in town, unpacks his books, does
his work, and then sleeps with his fathers.
"He cometh up and is cut down like a
flower; he fleeth as it were a shadow, and
never continueth in one stay." But Jesus
Christ is the same yesterday, to-day, and
forever. He is with his people even unto
the end of the world.

When Jesus handed over to Simon Peter
the charge of the Christian church, he
was careful to use the possessive pronoun "my." "Feed my lambs! Tend my
sheep! Feed my sheep!" It is the mightiest pronoun in the New Testament for the
saving of the minister from lordliness.
"Simon, son of Jonas, feed my lambs.
They are not yours, they are mine, but I
wish you to look after them for a little
while. Tend my sheep. They are not
yours. I do not give them to you. They
belong to me. Mine they always shall remain, but I ask you to tend them for a sea-

son for me. Feed my sheep. They are not yours. Not one of them shall ever pass from my possession, but I am going away for a few days, and I leave them with you. Guard them, feed them, guide them, be good to them for my sake. Follow me. Remember my gentleness, my watchfulness, my considerateness, my patience, my compassion, my readiness to help, my swiftness to heal, my gladness to sacrifice. Be the kind of shepherd to my lambs and my sheep that I have been to you. Follow me!"

V

The Shepherd's Reward

A CERTAIN school of ethics would question the wisdom of adding this subject to our list. "Virtue is its own reward," we are told, "and to inquire what one is going to get for doing his duty is vitiating. Work is better and the heart is nobler when one gives no thought to the recompense of his toil. We ought to do what we do with an eye single to the doing of it, with no demand for or anticipation of pay." It is a lofty-sounding philosophy, but it is too high-flown for healthy-minded mortals. It is an idol of the den. The New Testament knows nothing of the danger of looking to the end. Jesus never shrank from talking about results. For the joy that was set before him he endured the cross, despising the shame. In the presence of his disciples

he prayed, " I glorified thee on the earth,
and now, Father, glorify thou me." The
prophet declared that the Messiah would
see the travail of his soul and be satisfied.

In all his teachings Jesus leaves no un-
finished pictures. If he paints a sower
sowing seed, he paints also the harvest
growing golden in the sun. If he pictures
wheat and tares, he also pictures the barn
and the fire. If he sketches men working
in a vineyard, he sketches them at evening
time receiving, each man, his wages. When
he portrays Dives at the banquet, he is careful to tell what Dives deserves and gets.
He does not fail to inform us what is the
ultimate fate of the men entrusted with the
talents. He gives men reasons for doing
well, and assures them that they are going
to receive praise or condemnation according to their deeds. When Peter asked Jesus
what he was going to receive by way of recompense for the sacrifices he had made,
Jesus did not rebuke him but assured him
that " there is no man that hath left house,

or brethren, or sisters, or mother or father, or children, or lands, for my sake, and for the gospel's sake, but he shall receive a hundred fold now in this time, houses, and brethren, and sisters, and mothers, and children, and lands, with persecutions, and in the world to come eternal life." What does this mean but that the ministers of Christ are to be richly rewarded for their labors? They are to receive the very best things in this world and still better things in the next. What is promised is in every generation beautifully fulfilled.

A minister who does his work with an eye single to God's glory, leaving everything else behind, receives the best things the world affords. A multitude of people become his relatives and friends. Fathers and mothers are as proud of him as though he were a member of their family. Old men look down on him lovingly as on a son. Young men look up to him reverently as to a father. Men of his own age love him as a brother. A large circle feel that in him

perience overtakes you. Do not be thrown
into panic because all men do not speak well
of you.   Do not cry and sob when you meet
with opposition in your parish. Do your
duty and you will stir up trouble, but you
will never be left without faithful hearts
to love you.   When you go into Gethsemane, friends will remain praying at the
gate, and if you die on the cross you will
carry into heaven with you the affection-
ate devotion of many loyal hearts.   There
is nothing more beautiful on this earth than
the love of a parish for a faithful pastor.

There are ministers now alive who feel
that it would be worth while to toil a thousand years to win such love as they have received.   The taunts of Pharisees and the
gibes of the chief rulers and the priests are
all forgotten by the man who has the affection of a multitude of friends.   The petty
criticism to which every man in public place
is of necessity subjected, counts for nothing in the long sweep of the years.   All
the hateful and stinging things which **are**

said by spiteful critics are only a few dark, evanescent bubbles borne on the bosom of a tide of love. When a pastor comes near the end of his career, he forgets all about the little gusts of bitterness which have now and then blown across his path, and says with the Psalmist: "Goodness and mercy have followed me all the days of my life."

This love of the pastor is not only beautiful but lasting. It survives when many things else have perished. The affection for a pastor is different from the admiration for a preacher. The preacher, if eloquent, gets brass bands and torchlight processions. He is given newspaper space and applauding crowds, but his fame is speedily forgotten. When his vocal chords fail the crowds disappear, and only here and there is a heart which feels the sense of bereavement. Not so is it with the pastor. He lives in the hearts of those he has befriended. There is no memory so long-lived as the memory of kindness. Great pulpit efforts are speedily forgotten, fa-

when we meditate upon them the heavens open and the angels of God come down.

It is a commendable ambition to wish to live in the hearts of our fellows. The surest way of fulfilling that ambition is to do faithfully a shepherd's work. Many of us cannot be brilliant—we could have been had God so ordered—but we can every one be faithful. We can all be full of helpfulness, we can all have it said of us as it was said of Barnabas, " He was a good man and full of the Holy Ghost." We can all deserve to have chiseled on our tomb the simple inscription which is to be seen on a solitary grave at the foot of the Apennines : " He was a good man and a good guide."

In addition to the love of human beings the pastor receives other satisfactions even higher and more blessed. He has the gratification of helping people, the peace of mind which comes at the end of work by which a heart has been soothed and brightened, the pleasure of taking men by the hand and lifting them out of the sloughs of

the richest of all the gifts of heaven, and
this is peculiarly the gift granted to the
shepherd. By coming close to the individual soul the shepherd communicates to that
soul something of the essence of his own
spirit, and from that time forward he lives
not only in himself but also in another soul
which by him has been transfigured. He
is permitted by the goodness of God to
kindle a fire on an altar that was cold, and
re-create the world for a heart that had lost
the joy of living. Through his patience and
wisdom and fidelity men who have lived
without hope and without God in the world
are quickened into new life and begin to
glorify their Father who is in heaven. This
reward is richer than the first. It is a
great thing to win love for oneself, but
it is a greater thing to win love for God.
The shepherd can do both. Men will love
him as they love no other man in all the
world because he has taught them how to
love God. Things which eye saw not and
which ear heard not and which entered not

into the heart of man, but which were prepared for those who work for God, are revealed by the Eternal Spirit to the shepherd heart. The peace that passes understanding is a rich part of a shepherd's pay.

But while the pastor may receive these rich interior rewards, does he not buy them at the price of pulpit efficiency? While he is winning the affection of sundry persons whom he has individually befriended, is he not likely to lose his grip on the crowd? Many a young minister goes into his first parish feeling that every hour devoted to pastoral work is lost time. He does such work grudgingly, assuming that it is done at the expense of pulpit power. The assumption is mistaken. No man can study all the time. A few hours a day with books will exhaust the most vigorous brain. One can get more out of books in a half day than in a whole day, provided he uses the other half day in a way to sharpen his appetite for fresh reading. Moreover, in pastoral service a minister is at work on his sermon.   Sermon preparation has two stages—work on the preacher and work on the message.   The first is as important as the second.   If the preacher is not prepared the message will be thin.   The more thoroughly cultivated the heart of the preacher, the finer will be the texture and flavor of the sermon.   There is no preparation of the preacher comparable with that which he gets in mingling with people.   A minister is as truly fitting himself to preach when engaged in pastoral labors as when in his study he has his dictionaries and encyclopedias and commentaries spread out before him.

But is not close contact with the people disillusioning, and thereby injurious to the preacher's enthusiasm?   Does not distance lend enchantment to the view, and is not a more intimate knowledge of the pettinesses and meannesses of men apt to chill a speaker's zeal and introduce a pessimistic note into his message?   In this case is not a little knowledge a desirable thing, and a more

extensive knowledge somewhat dangerous?
These assumptions are all incorrect. It is
when we touch men with our finger-tips
that we dislike them. It is when we know
them only a little that we are harshest in
our judgments. When we come to know
them better we discover many good things
which we had missed at first. When we
understand all which they have suffered,
we make allowances for their shortcomings,
and our heart goes out in sympathy instead
of condemnation. Why, moreover, should
a minister be estranged by the moral infirmities of men? Why should he be galled
by their ignorance, or disgusted by their
foibles, or enraged by their prejudices, or
soured by their vices? If humanity were
morally sound, then were there no need of
a physician. If men were what they ought
to be, there would be no place for pastors.
It is because men are in a state of ruin that
Christ has sent his messengers throughout
the world. If a minister finds himself
growing cynical, let him drop his pen and

which mortals live. The greatest of all poets, Shakespeare, had a practical, matter-of-fact mind. He could interest himself in prosaic matters in little Stratford as well as poetic matters on the London stage. His mind was wide enough to take in the tragic experiences of the heroes and heroines of human history as well as the common work and play of obscure men in English village life. It was because he looked so sympathetically on the plain humdrum life about him that he was able to create characters which will be the joy of the world forever.

Some one may ask whether it is wise for a minister who wishes to become an author to give much time to ordinary pastoral duties. Why not? Doing pastoral work does not fit every man to be an author, for God in his mercy has not ordained that every minister shall write a book. But if a minister is sent into this world to write a book, his pastoral work will only increase his talent. No man has a right to publish a book unless he has learned something which

But suppose one has an unsocial nature, and finds pastoral work a burden, shall he coddle himself and let the lambs and sheep suffer? No. If the minister is lacking in social gifts, let him cultivate the social side of his nature more assiduously. If a man has one shoulder higher than the other, the thing to do is not to grow more lopsided, but by systematic exercises to bring the lower shoulder up. If a man is timid and awkward in conversation, let him converse more frequently. If he likes subjects better than men, as Nathaniel Burton confessed that he did, let him cultivate men more and more. No effective preacher can be a hermit. When a preacher lives an isolated life, the note of solitariness reports itself in his sermons. An unsocial minister needs to be born again. Why preach the new birth when you do not believe it a possible experience for yourself? Why extol the privilege of becoming a new man in Christ, if you persist in remaining the old man, making it impossible for God to work in you any mighty works because of your unbelief?

But can any man be a good preacher and a good pastor at the same time? Does not one gift kill the other? Does not the development of one capacity cause the atrophy of the other? There are ministers who look with jealous eye on their pastoral instincts, fearing that these, if allowed to grow, will paralyze the tongue for preaching. A minister sometimes shrinks from being called a " good pastor," fearing that the compliment disparages him as a preacher, and compromises him in the eyes of the public. Such men are deluded. Unless the parish is too large, a minister can be good both as pastor and preacher. The better he is as a pastor, the more effective he will be, other things being equal, as a preacher. It is because men limp and crawl in pastoral work that they often stumble and fall in the pulpit. Because they desert the people through the week, God deserts them on Sunday. A man cannot be an ideal preacher unless he has a shepherd heart.

Here then is a third reward which comes to shepherds, an increase of pulpit power. It is not claimed that every man who proves himself a faithful shepherd will become a famous pulpit orator. Pulpit orators are few—possibly because they are not essential to the progress of the church, and too many of them would corrupt the world. All that is here said is that pastoral work does not snuff out the preaching instinct, and that every man is all the better preacher because of the pastoral work he does, provided that this work is kept within proper limits. It may be profitable to note a few of the many services which pastoral work renders to the preacher. If some of you have high ambitions to conquer communities as sons of thunder, it will help you to escape the sin of doing pastoral work with a surly heart to remember what important and constant contributions pastoral work is making to your sermons. You ought never to do pastoral work grudgingly or of necessity, for God loves a cheerful pastor, and so do the people. Baxter called the pastoral work " a sweet and acceptable employment." The labors of a shepherd were to him " not burdens but mercies and delights." No wonder God's work prospered in his hands.

These are a few of the things which pastoral work does for the preacher. It supplies him with material for his sermons. A man who speaks every week to the same people year after year needs an enormous amount of material. It can be gotten out of the parish. The manna falls every day, and it falls near the minister's door. Fresh evidences of the malignity of sin are always being presented. Additional proofs of the presence and guidance of God are every day forthcoming. The best apology for the Christian religion cannot be gotten out of books, but must be framed out of material supplied by the people. The Sea of Galilee is in every parish, and Jesus walks along its shore, and talks with men and helps them as in the days of old. The minister ought to be there and listen to what the Lord is saying in the experiences of the people. It is there that one enters into the deep things of life. There are two kinds of profundities, book profundities and every-day profundities. What is matter? What is the relation of matter to spirit? What is the origin of evil? How can the human will be free? What is a tenable definition of inspiration? These are the profundities of the books, but the profundities of everyday life are deeper. Love and hate, hope and fear, faith and doubt, sin and duty, forgiveness and remorse, de-pression and aspiration—into all these the man who would preach with moving power must enter. It is amazing how many in-teresting things are being said every day in every parish, and the preacher ought to hear as many of them as possible: orig-inal things said by little children, and wise sayings of aged men and saintly women.

preached all he knows. The crock has been skimmed so often that no more cream will rise. The tree has been so often shaken that no more fruit will fall. Whenever these barren times arrive, let the minister lock up his study and go forth as a shepherd. Let him walk through his parish, observing what is going on. Let him talk with the people who are bearing the burden in the heat of the day. He will find, perhaps, a business man driven almost to despair by some sudden reverse in fortune, or some woman who is grieving herself into atheism over the death of a child, or some young man who is just entering upon a path that leads down to death, or some young woman who is all perplexed in her first efforts to live a Christian life—and when he gets home he will be in possession of a message. When a preacher finds himself with nothing to say it is because his heart is empty, and the thing to do is to go to the ocean of human need and fill it up again. A preacher always has something to say if he really knows his people.

It is in pastoral work that the minister comes to know human nature. His parish is the human soul edited up to date. It is not enough to know what the world needs, one must know what it wants. Wants and needs aɩe not the same, and the preacher must know both. It is not sufficient to know the good things which are being said in the parish, one ought to know some of the foolish things also, the vices as well as the virtues, the errors as well as the truths. The weaknesses as well as the strong points of the people ought to be clearly apprehended. It is only when the preacher is possessed of this knowledge that he can preach with greatest effect. No rifleman is likely to hit the target if he fires in the dark. How can a preacher aim a sermon if he does not know where the people are? It is as important that a minister should know his congregation as it is that he should know his Bible. How can he know his congregation unless he meets the people one by one? Walter Scott made it a practice always to talk with every man with

whom he was casually thrown. He loved
to talk to his servants and the servants of
his friends—gardeners, coachmen, footmen,
all sorts of men were interesting to him.
A servant of his once declared that " Sir
Walter speaks to every man as if he was
his blood relation." No wonder Scott became a wizard who charmed the hearts of
millions. By coming close to the human
heart, he understood its beat; and when the
Waverley novels appeared, men high and
low felt in them the beating of a heart like
their own. The minister who would be an
effective preacher must speak to every man
as if that man were his blood relation.
Truth is to be applied—how can it be applied to men in the dark? Knowledge is
to be used—how can it be used wisely unless one knows the people who are in need
of it? Everything depends on the point of
contact, and this is established in pastoral
work. Matthew Arnold used to call Shelley
" a beautiful and ineffectual angel beating
in the void his luminous wings in vain."

or the Latin or the German or the French, when a plain English word would do his work better. Every opaque word subtracts from the preacher's power. A preacher's vocabulary ought to be subjected to the refining influence of ordinary conversation. It is in the suds of everyday speech that the starch of the schools must be washed out of the preacher's style. Style has a tendency to stiffen, and sentences, unless watched, have a fashion of becoming elaborate and complex. If the preacher has fine literary taste he will be tempted to indulge in minute touches, in dainty allusions, in exquisite and intricate phrasings, and in all those delicate gradations of light and shade which are the delight of the exceptional and fastidious and highly cultivated mind. Before he knows it his style will be a barrier between the people and his truth. The sheep will look toward those wonderful and beautiful sentences, but they will not be fed. Every preacher needs the disciplinary castigation of conversation with common people. In conversation one is obliged to be sensible. He cannot put on a silly and artificial tone. If he did, others would laugh at him and he would probably laugh at himself. If certain preachers could hear their pulpit tones, they would be exceedingly amused. When we converse, our words are simple and short, our sentences are straight and direct, our style is flexible, and hence conversation with plain people is one of the best schools for the cultivation of an effective pulpit style. The bane of the pulpit is complex sentences, artificial arrangement of clauses, and a style that is so elaborate that the attention flags in trying to extract the thought from it. All these are burnt up in the fire of conversation. A sermon is defective if it sounds bookish. It is best when it is nearest friendly and unstudied talk. Daily intercourse with all sorts of people will do more to keep a minister off his pulpit stilts than anything else. Samuel Johnson at the age of thirty-five wrote the life of his friend

object. Wordsworth always kept his eye on the object. That is one reason why Dryden is unread and Wordsworth is just coming to his own. Preachers often preach with their eye off the people. This is evident from their language. No man with his eye on the people could possibly go on using a style which is found in many pulpits. Walter Bagehot gives ministers a dig when he says of Coleridge: "Like a Christian divine he did not regard persons. He went right on, not knowing what was going on in other people's minds." This is a defect which may be remedied by conversing in the homes of the people. Personal intercourse gives directness to thought and clearness to speech. In conversation style always particularizes, and language fits down snug round the individual mind. The preacher who is willing to let his people talk to him through the week will know better how to talk to them on Sunday.

There are still more important things to be gotten from the people—originality, vividness, fire, and the ring of reality. A preacher is nothing if not interesting. An uninteresting sermon is a bore. It is not enough, as some imagine, that a sermon be true, it must be true and also interesting. What matters it whether it be true or not if people will not listen to it, and they certainly will not listen to it unless it is interesting. A minister who cannot preach interesting sermons was never intended for the pulpit. The first duty of the preacher is to get the attention, and if he cannot get it he might as well go home. Now to be interesting a sermon must be original, vivid, and sincere. How can a preacher be original, dealing as he must with themes worn threadbare with the handling of two thousand years? All the doctrines of the Christian faith are commonplaces, and every Christian precept is familiar to everybody. How then can a sermon be original? Originality lies in the accent with which the sermon is spoken, in the fire in which the sermonic elements have been fused, in the application which the preacher makes of the truth to the people in that particular parish. A man to preach with originality must have first-hand knowledge of the things of which he speaks. He must look upon the world with his own eyes. He must know men at first hand. He must grapple with sin in his own heart and in the hearts of his people. He must know the joys and sorrows, the temptations and triumphs, of the Christian life. Every man is original who drinks at the fountains of the world's life and does not rely on the cisterns which we call books. The man who mingles with men, and plays with children, and who knows what is going on in his parish, will have a vitality and fresh- ness in his speech which will compel people to listen. His thoughts will have a peculiar edge, his message will be vivid. One can- not make a sermon vivid by picking out of the dictionary lurid and picturesque words. A vivid sermon comes out of a feeling heart. A heart that has heat can make dull words incandescent. How can a minister scorch cruelty and injustice unless he has seen them face to face in his own parish? How can he abhor the liquor traffic until he has worked with men whom the saloon has finally dragged down to hell? It is first-hand experience with sin which enables men to preach about it, and it is first-hand experience with Christ which makes it possible to tell the old, old story in phrases that etch themselves in fire upon the heart. Men who hold aloof from the everyday life and suffering of the world may pretend emotion and mimic passion, but their sermons lack the note of reality, and the congregation sits unmoved. A man to be a preacher must have an experiencing nature. He must live over in himself the joys and sorrows through which his people pass. He must think with them, feel with them, suffer with them, rejoice with them—only so can the gospel come from his lips with power. "I preached what I felt," said John Bunyan. His ex-

gether by young men whose salary depends on their ability to make an interesting story. The average paper gives a picture of the world which is lurid, exaggerated, out of proportion, and in false perspective. The world is not half so bad or hopeless as the average paper would make it seem, and the minister needs to correct the newspaper picture by intimate contact with his parish. Some ministers are scandalously pessimistic in their preaching. In the paper one sees chiefly the bad, but in the parish one sees the good as well as the bad—so much of the good that one can thank God and take courage. The theological magazines and the books of biblical criticism deal with a group of problems of great interest to limited circles. The minister who gives too much time to these problems is likely to put an exaggerated emphasis on their importance. The latest theory of a daring German professor, the last speculation of a Dutch or French savant, looms large in the vision of the minister, and he burns, if a conservative, with holy zeal to demolish these new enemies of the faith; or, if he be a radical, to communicate this new-found truth to his people. When the minister comes from the last theological magazine all aglow with enthusiasm over some new interpretation, or with indignation over some wild speculation, let him take a walk through his parish and note how indifferent men are to these theological storms. The foolish things in the magazines will never reach his people unless he tells them. The predicted collapse of time-honored doctrines will never pain them if he keeps still. Plausible theories now dominant, but which will be antiquated ten years from now, will not disturb the souls of the faithful if he does not hurl thunder-bolts at them from the pulpit. When one sees a minister demolishing a foreign critic of whom his people have never heard, and demonstrating the falsity of a theory of which his people have never dreamed, and laboriously striving to clear away in a course of six ser-

them confidence in him and to lead them to feel that he has a manly and brotherly heart. Building up in men a responsive disposition, creating in them a friendly and hospitable attitude, this is work which the minister as shepherd does, getting them ready for the message of the minister as prophet. The work of the prophet is to transmit, to convey a message to others. In the transfer of a truth from one man to another, two things are of supreme importance. The first is that the preacher has a grip on it himself, and the second is that the hearer get a grip on it too. To be sure that the hearer gets a grip on the truth, it is necessary for the preacher to know the hearer's exact position. Treasures cannot be safely handed to men in the dark. The truth which the minister conveys is not to stop with the man who receives it, it is by him to be handed on. A preacher never reaches his highest success unless his people repeat his sermons. When they re-preach his message, his power is increased

fitted to speak of God whom he has not seen.

The highest reward of the shepherd is an increase in spiritual stature. Character is the greatest of all treasures, and character is built by action. It is the things which one does which determine what he is. "Character forms itself in the stream of the world." A minister's character is formed in the stream of parish life. It is the things which he does rather than the books which he reads which mold his temper and fashion his disposition. It is his work as a shepherd rather than his message as a prophet which has most to do with the enriching of his heart and the refining of his spirit. The reward of the shepherd is that he becomes increasingly like the good shepherd, he is transformed into the same image from glory to glory even as from the Lord the Spirit. The minister who watches and guards and guides men, heals and rescues and feeds them, develops by his work the virtues and graces of the Saviour himself. What saint is more beautiful in his old age than the man who for forty or fifty years has done faithfully the work of the shepherd? One star differs from another in glory, and so do the types of sainthood differ from one another. But for tenderness of heart, and beauty of soul, and Christlikeness of spirit, what character known among men surpasses that of the shepherd saint?

The shepherd life cultivates a sensitiveness in all the nerves of feeling. The sympathies grow broad, the heart expands and takes in classes which were at first shut out. There is something in preaching which tends to make a man intolerant. One can be so loyal to what he thinks to be the truth as to become hard of heart toward those who will not receive it. Again and again in Christian history the sad spectacle has been presented of a man really entrusted with a message from heaven, but whose fiery devotion to truth closed his heart against those who did not agree with

him. The work of the shepherd ever tends
to mellow and widen the heart. Working
with the lambs, caring for the sick, rescuing the lost, feeding the hungry, all this
adds new breadth to the sympathy and
helps one to enter more completely into
the lives of others. A shepherd whose life
has been faithful is sure to be genial in his
judgments and indulgent in the allowances
which he makes for all classes of men.
The shepherd grows in patience. As long
as he lives, his work makes heavy demands
on his powers of endurance, but they re-
spond to the call. The work of a shepherd
is full of interruptions, vexations, and dis-
appointments, but these try his soul and
refine it. The precipitate hastiness of the
earlier years gives way to calm deliber-
ativeness, and the feverish irritability of
youth is replaced by the cool strength of
forbearance. In working with human nature a man gets something of the patience
of a mother. He is not daunted by a score
of failures. He does not surrender to ap-

ing realization of its immeasurable power throws the shepherd back on God in Christ. Faith takes a deepening meaning. He understands as few men do that it is necessary to walk by faith. He learns also why Paul calls hope a helmet, for he knows that without hope he cannot hold his head up in the battle. He comes to know as few men know the length and breadth and height and depth of Christian love. He reads as few men know how to read Paul's immortal words: " Love suffereth long and is kind; love beareth all things, believeth all things, hopeth all things, endureth all things." There are many things which a faithful shepherd must endure, and when crucified he prays with Jesus: " Father, forgive them, for they know not what they do." The faithful shepherd comes to know the fellowship of Christ's sufferings, becoming conformable to his death. One may be a student and a scholar and write ponderous books of wisdom, and never once know the meaning of Gethsemane. One may work glowing ideas into golden speech, and thrill men's hearts with a tongue which has the wizardry of genius, and never understand the significance of the cross. But when one becomes a shepherd and gives his life to shepherding men, he begins at once to be baptized with the baptism that Jesus was baptized with and to drink the cup which Jesus drank. It is not until one comes out of the library and gets down beside some one who has fallen and is bleeding and half dead, that one becomes a man of sorrows and acquainted with grief. If to be Christlike is the greatest of all privileges, then that privilege belongs preëminently to the shepherd.

It is a reward that is offered to all shepherds, no matter how large or how small may be their flock. There is no parish in any part of the world so small or so obscure that it does not furnish room for the growing of a shepherd saint. John Fletcher was pastor for twenty-five years in the little village of Madeley, and he grew

there into a saint whose name will be
fragrant forever. The brilliant Oxford
scholar, John Keble, was for thirty years
the pastor of the little village of Hursley,
and in that quiet country town he grew to
be so much like Jesus that many men declared him to be the saintliest man they had
ever known. When God distributes his
rewards he does not ask a minister concerning the size of his parish, but simply in regard to the spirit with which he has done
his work. To every man who shepherds
Christ's sheep is the privilege granted of
growing into the likeness of the perfect
shepherd. Large parishes spoil some men,
but small parishes spoil others. High
positions are dangerous, and so also are
positions which are humble. A prominent
church may make the minister conceited,
but an obscure church may do the same
thing. A man in a humble parish may become very conscious of the sacrifice he is
making and talk about it often. Those who
are very conscious of their sacrifice, and

We have come at last to the crowning
reward, everlasting fellowship with Jesus
Christ and unending participation in his
glory. Whatever the glory of the Chief
Shepherd is, we who are under-shepherds
are, if faithful, to share in it. His prayer
was and is, " I will that where I am there
they may be also, that they may behold my
glory." What that glory is we know not
now, but we shall know hereafter. Paul
calls it a " crown of righteousness." Peter
calls it a " crown of glory." Jesus calls it
a " joy." The idea of sharing the life of
Jesus Christ himself was the one which
sustained Paul in all his tribulations. In
the Roman prison he kept repeating to himself phrases such as these: " If we died
with him, we shall also live with him: if
we endure, we shall also reign with him."
This expectation was foundationed on the
words of Jesus himself. To a company of
drooping and doleful shepherds he said
on the night of his betrayal: " I go to prepare a place for you, and if I go and pre-

pare a place for you, I will come again and receive you unto myself, that where I am there ye may be also." John, exiled on the Isle of Patmos, looking out upon a storm-swept world, the scattered Christian congregations burning like candles in the gale, is not daunted by the present tragedy and disaster, but hears, above the crash and thunder of the tempest, a divine voice saying: "He that overcometh I will give to him to sit down with me in my throne, as I also overcame and sat down with my father in his throne."